Sam by Roy Grantham

Published in 2022 by FeedARead Publishing
Copyright © Roy Grantham as named on the book cover.

Thanks to Raoul Grantham for his great cover design
Thanks to Mariette Grantham for her proof reading

Roy Grantham

By the same author:-

Trouble in the Family

Little Beechdown

Death without Dying

The Boy in the Red Sweater

The boy Who Came in from the Cold

The Gardener

The Book Club

Deeds and Mideeds

The Shoe

Butterly Hall

Ma Blackstock's Place

An Ordinary Life

Sam by Roy Grantham

If you want to make God laugh, tell him your plans.

In such small deceits begin the auction of our souls.

Living's more difficult than Sanskrit or chemistry or economics.

How small of all that human hearts endure
That part which laws or kings can cause or cure.

Chapter 1

He walked with a forward motion, his long legs striding out and his head bobbing up and down with each stride. No wonder the kids at the school where he'd taught for a short while had christened him hopalong Cassidy which soon became Hoppy. He had the academic qualifications to be a teacher yet neither the temperament nor the aptitude required to do the job. The kids found him easy meat when it came to class discipline, and it was quickly obvious that his lack of control meant that learning was pushed to one side by the master's struggle for control with his unruly pupils.

Maggie loved him because despite, what some might have said were his physical oddities, he was at heart a kind and gentle man who would never hurt a fly. She had first met him when she went into the council offices to pay a parking fine. Trylon Makepeace, which was Hoppy's real name, was sympathetic and joked with Maggie about the unfairness of how she'd been caught in default of the law by an eager traffic warden. For some reason their mutual smiles exchanged messages and when Trylon said he had a break coming up did she fancy a coffee in the local coffee bar she smilingly accepted his invitation. Tentatively they asked each other questions about their personal lives. They were both in their forties and past the age of instant expectation yet there was a sense of mutuality that presaged well for future friendship, probably more important than passion although neither would have used those words.

"Where do you live Trylon?"

That led on to a conversation about their individual living arrangements. Both had small rented flats, both lived quiet lives. Hoppy with his boring job in the council offices and Maggie as a teaching assistant at the local primary school. The truth was that Trylon could have afforded to buy a house if he so desired. His mum had had him rather late in life, doted on him and left him a legacy when she died, the father having vanished into the ether many years ago.

These two people who some would describe as just past their prime, quietly, and without much passion, decided to live together. They liked each other which was of course vital to their relationship. They didn't see any need to formalise their arrangement through marriage although when Maggie became pregnant, they decided it was the right thing to do. The couple were excited at the prospect of becoming parents. They were excited by the process of buying a small semi-detached house on the outskirts of Exeter. What had been a pretty dull life for these two forty-something-year-olds had now become a wonderland of new experiences. If either of them had been asked whether they were in love with the other they would certainly have hesitated before answering, yet their relationship worked well. Two considerate people, two people who you could say were almost amazed at the prospect that were going to produce a new being into the world, a baby no less.

Their wedding at the Registry Office was a quiet affair as became the quiet couple. Trylon had his brother

Joseph there and a couple of friends from the office while Maggie invited her mother and sister and her best friend Sarah. The ceremony didn't last long and soon they were all having drinks in the Green Dragon before sitting down to lunch in an atmosphere of pleasant socialising. Simon, one of Trylon's friends from work, did eventually get to his feet to toast the happy couple and Trylon made a stuttering effort to reply. That formality out of the way the newly weds went on their way to spend a few days down in Cornwall for their honeymoon.

Six months later a baby girl, whose ecstatic parents decided to call Samantha, was born. "She'll be called Sam but I don't mind that and nor will she I predict." A tired but smiling Maggie held up the baby for Tri to introduce himself. She's been calling him Tri ever since their relationship had become close enough for that sort of thing. He gazed down at the red and somewhat wrinkled miniature face that looked back at him with what seemed to be an air of bright-eyed surprise.

"She's beautiful," said Trylon handing her gently back to the open arms of her mum.

Thereafter what turned out to be a pretty baby was spoiled something rotten. She turned out to be a good baby anyway, sleeping a lot and making few demands on her mother. After six months Maggie went back to work after finding a suitable nursery where she was confident her little girl would be happy. As she got older Samantha began to reveal a personality beyond her years. She was a hit at her primary school even though one or two of the kids might have thought she was a limelight stealer. She was into learning the little songs from school then showing them off to her parents at home or to visitors although there weren't many of those except for Grace, Maggie's mother, who had been head over heels in love with the child ever since she'd been born.

As Sam grew older she found making friends came easily to her – she had an inherent liking for people, even those she hardly knew – it was as natural to her as breathing. Once she'd started at secondary school she was always asking Maggie if she could invite a friend for a sleep-over and of course there was reciprocation. The child was so full of energy. Maggie was exhausted just watching her. There was always something she wanted to do, somewhere she wanted to go. She enjoyed school and without ever appearing to do much homework she got good marks. Her parents were pleased of course but neither of them were really au fait with the latest teaching methods despite Trylon's time as a teacher.

Would it have been unkind to refer to Samantha as precocious? Perhaps but any worrying actions were always accompanied by that winsome charm that came so naturally to her. On one occasion she had arranged to stay overnight with Fey whose family lived only two streets away. For some reason Maggie needed to talk to her daughter so rang the number she'd been given only to find that Samantha wasn't there. There was a bit of a panic involving ringing round other numbers before she found Sam was staying with Jennifer and had forgotten to tell her mum of the changed arrangements.

Yet you just couldn't be angry with the child. Any chastisement bounced off her like hail on a tin roof. She would look at her mother with those shining green eyes whenever a scolding appeared on the horizon and that was it. No more to be said except that she was sorry and it wouldn't happen again. She meant it at the time but truth was that she was rather careless when it came to considering Maggie's feeling and her worries. Her self-confidence was so powerful that she couldn't see why anyone should worry about little things like where she was and who she was with. She might have said when asked that she was quite capable of looking after herself and there was no need for anyone to worry. She enjoyed using her computer and spent hours on facebook, Instagram and other sites her parents had never heard of. The photograph she used for her online activities showed a beautiful young lady eager to chat so it was no wonder her Facebook list of friends was large and growing by the day. Yet those good marks at school kept appearing despite Trylon's worries about whether or not she was doing her homework.

At fifteen Sam had her first sexual encounter. It was with a boy from another Exeter school, the brother of one of Sam's classmates with whom she had arranged a sleep over. It wasn't much of an encounter and never got round to actual penetration, but it reinforced her ideas about the power her body could have over members of the opposite sex. Simon was the boy's name and he was keen to meet up again, to do it properly this time, he said. Sam shied away much to the lad's annoyance. From her point of view it had only been the convenience of opportunity that had caused her to try out sex for the first time. She didn't really fancy Simon if the truth be told and if she were to experiment further it would be with a boy she did fancy.

That Particular boy didn't come into the picture until Sam had started on her A levels and even then she kept Timothy, as the boy was called, at arm's length until she was sure of her feelings towards him. They were both aiming to go to university to take a Psychology degree if they got the right A levels so they had that in common and spent quite a bit of time together both in class and out. When Tim asked her out for the first time, she said she had too much work to do and no time for dating. Then being the soft-hearted girl she was she relented after seeing the downcast expression on the lad's face. She would go to a disco with him although he shouldn't get any ideas about what she'd agreed to. On that first date Tim picked her up from home in his dad's car. Trylon and Maggie had obliquely raised matters of concern to parents of girls of Sam's age yet were impressed by the young man standing shyly in the hallway. Trylon asked a few questions about the boy's family while Maggie mentioned drinking and driving. However the overall impression they got was that here was a sensible young man who was not going to lead their precious daughter astray.

"Don't be too late darling," Maggie called as the young couple walked down the driveway. Then back inside. "Seems a nice enough boy doesn't he, Tri?"

It was as might be expected an energetic evening for the young couple during which there was a certain amount of 'getting to know you'. Some time before the disco was due to finish Sam accepted Tim's suggestion that they drive out to Backleigh Common for a breath of fresh air, a suggestion that neither of them believed for a moment was the true reason for their short journey. Their kissing quickly evolved into something more serious as Tim's passion and impatience grew. Soon they were out of the car and lying on a rug under the stars; all very romantic you might say, not that Sam was really concerned with romance. Her aim was to lose her virginity with the help of a boy she rather liked and recognised as a straight up guy. Romance was something you grew into she thought at least that's how she saw it. They did have brief sexual intercourse which left Sam wondering what all the fuss was about. Tim appeared deflated and when, after a break, he suggested they do it again, Sam said she thought she'd better be getting back home as her mum would be worrying her socks off.

So that was Sam, aged eighteen, losing her maidenhood just for the hell of it, and perhaps to start her breakaway from the rather stilted boundaries set by her parents. She loved them both, but they had little to do with her life as it would be once she started at university. As far as Tim was concerned, well he had done his job. She remained friends but there were no more tristes beneath the stars much to the poor boy's abject disappointment. They were heading for different universities anyway so their friendship at any level would be coming to an end before the end of the year.

To Sam that summer appeared to be a transition between childhood and becoming a woman. Nothing to do with age particularly, it was more that she saw ahead a time when the tender love of Maggie and Trylon could be put on hold while she found her own personality, made her own discoveries and relied on her own resources.

It was a happy summer for the sun-gold girl with the flying hair, making the most of it usually in the company of her friend Kitty Belston. She played tennis, she went swimming in the outdoor pool at the club her parents had signed her up for. She went to gigs and spent time at discos. And all the time she was getting her mind adjusted to her life ahead. She was no longer a virgin but that in no way made her sexually active. She went on lots of dates with boys but they never came to anything. On one occasion when she was sharing a tent with Kitty at a music festival she engaged in a brief bout of kissing with her friend and for a few short seconds wondered if her proclivities lay towards her own sex but it didn't lead to anything and she quickly put such an idea out of her mind.

Tim had done his duty you might say and had now drifted into history.

Chapter 2

When the time came to say goodbye to Kitty she was sad in the moment yet was quickly restored to a positive mood by the excitement of her trip up to Sheffield. Her mum and dad insisted on accompanying her to make sure she settled into her room in the halls of residence. When Sam finally managed to persuade her loving parents that it was time to start their long journey back to Devon she felt an immense weight lifted off her shoulders. She loved them to pieces but now was a new stage in her life, one she must navigate on her own.

"That your mum and Dad was it? Bit of a relief isn't it? I'm Jemma by the way." A dark curly-haired girl of Sam's age stood at the door grinning in a friendly way.

Sam smiled in return, introduced herself, and invited Jemma into her room. "Actually they're lovely but just for now I need some space of my own if you know what I mean."

"Don't I just." Jemma's throaty chuckle confirmed her understanding of exactly what Sam meant. "What course are you taking at this venerable institution?"

They were going to get on Sam felt sure. This girl was full of fun, a sense of humour to go with her ease of manner. "Boring I'm afraid. Philosophy, the fallback for us lot that don't really know what they want to do, but are certain of one thing and that's to escape from home and hearth."

"What say we investigate the student bar, get thoroughly pissed to celebrate our newfound freedom?" The immediate affinity between the two girls was spontaneous yet real for all that. They ran down the corridor together like two gazelles being chased by a leopard or perhaps just two young girls each happy to have found a friend so early in their new academic life. The bar wasn't crowded that first evening, but it didn't take long before the new friends were joined by a couple of boys looking for early and maybe easy pick-ups – in the nicest way of course.

"Hello girls what you drinking then? I'm Ben by the way and this layabout is Matthew known to his friends, few that they are, as Mat."

Sam and Jemma were fine with it. Afterall they were all students at a seat of learning weren't they and friendships between the alumni was certainly part of what it was all about. Mat was apparently the quiet one. While Ben went off to fetch another round of drinks, he didn't have much to say. A few questions about what the girls were studying and where they were from and that was it until Ben came back to add some sparkle to the party.

Ben sank a good quarter of his pint of beer before turning to grin at the two girls. "What you lassies going to sign up for then? There's quite a lot going on as you've probably seen on Facebook."

Sam shrugged. "Too much to take in, festivals, events, gigs, societies and all that. Need to give it some thought."

The youngsters put away several more drinks before Sam made it clear she'd had enough by producing a hardly disguised yawn and saying she was off to bed. Quick as a flash Ben offered to escort her back to her room. She shrugged, conscious that the lad was in for a disappointment when they got there. She let him kiss her goodnight before, after a minor struggle, she made it clear that she meant what she'd said about going to bed and strictly by herself.

Ben's face flashed a fleeting scowl before he remembered that there were other days and he shouldn't waste his efforts on what for the present anyway was a lost cause. "OK baby see you tomorrow, maybe help you decide on which of the opportunities on offer might suit you."

Sam slumped down on the bed and reached for her iPad to find the expected messages from her parents demanding a response on how she was settling in. Wearily she typed in a few platitudes and pressed 'send' before dragging off her clothes and after a brief visit to the bathroom snuggling down beneath the duvet for her first night of freedom. She lay there and let her thoughts drift through her mind in sleepy disarray before eventually slipping into a deep restful sleep.

In the morning when Sam surfaced form a deep sleep she didn't at first remember where she was. Then as it all came back to her she stretched out luxuriously and contemplated the days to come. Ben, who was into his second year, had filled her in with some of the things going on in Intro week and she couldn't wait to see what was on offer. Her inclination to lie and wallow in her warm comfortable bed was overtaken by the excitement of the new. She had just made herself some coffee when there was a knock at the door. There on the threshold was her new friend Jemma all bright-eyed and bushy-tailed and ready for action.

"You not dressed yet? I'll have one of those and then we're off to the student union building to see what's going on." She sat down on the bed Sam had recently vacated and grinned at Sam full of energy and enthusiasm. Under pressure from Jemma Sam had a quick shower in her minute bathroom, did something with her hair before pulling a pair of tight jeans, a loose top and her sheepskin jacket. There was a chill in the air and she hated to be cold. The two girls made their way over to the students' union building where the Activities fair was in full swing. Sam had slept longer than she'd intended and it was already eleven o'clock when they entered the bustling main hall. At first sight it looked chaotic, but soon they were to discover some order in the madness.

They set about all the various registration requirements. On top of the Main registration, there was module enrolment, university health service and welcome meetings.

After all that Jemma puffed out her cheeks and grinned at her new friend. "Tell you what Sam, next thing for me is to find some student friendly companies to see about getting a part-time job. Plenty of time to think about all the goodies on offer a bit later."

For the time being Sam didn't have money worries as grandma Grace had made a generous donation to her living expenses shortly before she'd left for her new life in Sheffield. As the morning went on, she wasn't altogether surprised when a grinning Ben turned up to renew their last night's acquaintance. She knew he fancied her and although she had absolutely no wish for anything serious it was good to make friends of both sexes so for now the boy's attentions were welcome. "Where's your mate then?"

Sam smiled. "Looking for a job over there." She gestured in the direction of the company stalls.

"Good luck with that. What say you and me take a stroll round, see what's on offer. I may be able to offer some advice, seasoned veteran that I am." There was that disarming grin again.

"No time for that yet Ben. As soon as Jemma's finished we're going to do all our enrolment stuff, register and all that, go to welcome meetings. Set up our computer accounts and so on. Ben looked crestfallen but soon perked up. "OK but once you've done all that I could show you the ropes if you like."

Sam liked the guy but wasn't going to be hurried through this exciting stage of her university life. "Slow down Ben, I've only just arrived and I want to see for myself what's on offer."

He sulked for a brief moment before his good nature came back to the fore. "Sure thing baby but I could be your guide. Without trying to interfere in any way, just as a mate."

"I think Jemma can do that but it's all right with me if you want to tag along."

"Your mate would be better off waiting until Thursday when there's a special day dedicated to job searching. Today is really about what the SU can do for you and what facilities it can offer. The whole thing goes on over two weeks you know with sports and activities and all sorts of freebies.

Jemma was still tied up looking for a job so Sam and Ben started to make their rounds through the stalls laid out in the students' union hall. They were mainly concerned with what the SU could offer the students, food and drink advice services and so on. When there was still no sign of Jemma they grabbed themselves a couple of pizzas one of which was free and some beer and found an unused table at the side of the hall where they sat down to eat their lunch. Sam was still on cloud 9 and while she liked the persistent Ben and welcomed him as a friend it wasn't him who was creating the state of euphoria in her mind, it was more the sense of freedom, of being her own mistress, of being in exciting new surroundings waiting for the next wonderful discovery to come along.

As they strolled outside the hall they met a couple of lads obviously friends of Ben's. "Getting in with the fresh stuff are you Ben?" It was a tall youth with what, to Sam, appeared to be a sardonic look on his face, who spoke.

Ben frowned and appeared about to say something like 'why don't you shut your face' but instead politely offered. "Hi chaps I'd like to introduce you to Samantha Makepeace part of this year's new intake. Sam these two reprobates go by the names of Douglas Templeton and Simon Norton." Just as they were shaking hands a smiling Jemma arrived on the scene and the introduction had to be gone though all over again.

"Tell you what girls what about coming to a party tonight, nothing special just some music and a few beers. If you're up for it Ben'll give you the address, might even give you a lift if you ask him sweetly."

Sam glanced at Jemma, accepted the slight nod. "Very kind, yes we'd love to come, might even bring a bottle of wine."

Ben was reluctant to say goodbye but the two girls, tired by what had already gone on that day opted for a few hours back in halls to rest up and have a cup of tea. The loyal Ben promised to pick them up at about nine o'clock to take them to the party.

Back in her room Sam threw herself down on her bed. Jemma had gone back to her own room to decide what to wear for the party although there were still hours to go. Sam's thoughts were scudding through her head at the prospect of days full of boys, parties and raves and before she knew she had drifted off to sleep. She awoke with a jerk, grabbed her cell to check the time and was relieved to see it was only 7 o'clock. She yawned, half wanting to go back to that delicious cocoon in which she'd been enveloped for the last hour or so. She shook her hair out of her eyes and made for the tiny shower cubicle to bring herself back to life before getting dressed in what she thought as party clothes, a short skirt with a peasant top which went well with her long fair hair.

Jemma knocked on her door well before the time Ben was due to pick them up. She looked gorgeous dressed in a loose-fitting dress, maybe more like a robe. She was grinning as she produced a half bottle of gin. "Thought it might get us in the mood before we enter the unknowns of the Sheffield uni social scene," she giggled. "Got any glasses?"

By the time Ben arrived on the scene the two girls had banished any nerves they might have had about the party to come. Ben was full of himself. Perhaps being the guy to bring two gorgeous birds to the party had something to do with it. The party was at the house rented by Douglas, Simon and a couple of other boys. When they got there it was already noisy, the music loud and the party goers taking advantage of the booze on offer although as yet it wasn't overcrowded.

Ben ushered the two girls into the room where the action was taking place. For the moment they all stood on the threshold uncertain about the etiquette of getting something to drink. Then before the three of them could get immersed in the party scene a short fat boy with glasses trundled up and in a loud voice exclaimed, "And where has this beautiful dusky maiden been all my life?"

Jemma turned rigid. "You sexist bastard, keep your comments to yourself." Her voice was loud enough to be heard over the sound of the music and gradually the party goers stopped their gyrations and turned to look towards the newcomers in the doorway.

"Hey look no offence meant, just a way of speaking." The boy who had turned bright red still stood there uncertain of what to do next.

"Trust you Piggy." A lone voice came from inside the room.

Ben who had been shocked by the comment and Jemma's reaction now came to life. If truth were known he didn't think Piggy's remark was particularly offensive but if Jemma was upset then he was here to see she got the respect she deserved.

"I think you owe this lady an apology Piggy you ignorant bastard."

The fat boy spluttered out the demanded apology whinging all the time that he was no racist and had meant no harm. Gradually the music started up again, the guests went back to their dancing while Ben rustled up some bottles of beer. The tension between the three youngsters lessaned as they moved into the room to watch the party scene and absorb the atmosphere. Piggy has disappeared and wasn't seen again that night. It had never crossed Sam's mind to think of Jemma as anything else but one more student new to university life just as she was. It wasn't long before both girls were dragged into the melee and the incident with Piggy was pushed into the background. Sam wasn't a drinker and even the few beers she drank left her feeling somewhat light-headed. When eventually she decided she'd had enough for one day Ben was happy to give the two girls a lift back to their halls of residence maybe hoping for more than he actually got. What he did get was the thanks of both girls and, after Jemma had tactfully gone into her room, an exchange of a few kisses before Sam pleaded tiredness and sent him on his way.

Ben gone, Sam slumped back on her bed to let her thoughts lazily recapture the events of what had been a very full day. She had almost dropped off to sleep when she was brought back to consciousness by a light knock on her door. There was Jemma, a slightly worried look on her face and perhaps a dampness about it that suggested earlier tears.

"Can I come in for a minute Sam. I expect you want to get to bed but I couldn't leave some things unsaid. I expect you think I over-reacted to that boy's comment about dusky maidens."

Sam put an arm round her new-found friend. "Just one ignorant bastard love, forget him, he doesn't represent anything."

"Oh but he does Sam. I was born in Bradford, my mum and dad were born in England, yet all my life I've had to put up with comments and insults referring to the fact that I'm black. Our multi-racial society in this country may be a fact, but it doesn't stop the inherent racism brooding beneath the surface." She stopped to let the tears run down her beautiful face.

"There'll always be bigots around but they don't represent the ordinary people in the street."

"I'm not so sure. Not so blatant as it was perhaps but always there lurking beneath the surface for many white people."

They talked on into the night until, tired to the bone, they slipped under Sam's duvet and fell asleep in each other's arms.

In the morning when Sam struggled into wakefulness Jemma had gone. Sam rubbed her eyes, yawning widely before glancing at her cell to see it was getting on for lunch time. She dragged herself out of the delicious warmth of her bed intending to take a shower. On the way she noticed a piece of paper lying on her desk. It read 'Thank you so much, you're lovely Sam.'

Well it was another day now, so a shower, followed by a mug of life- giving coffee. Then she dragged on a pair of jeans, slipped on a sweatshirt emblazoned across the front with 'peace' and, feeling a little chilly, added her denim jacket. She had half expected to find Ben knocking on her door. In his absence she decided to pay a call on her neighbour. There was no answer to her knock on Jemma's door and she turned away thinking she would venture over to the activities fair by herself. Not to be. As she walked down the corridor she heard a voice calling her name. There was sleepy0eyed Jemma looking as though she'd just woken up which in fact was the case.

"Sorry love, I was still well away. Why don't you come in while I make myself moderately presentable? It was shortly after that that the two girls set off once again for the activities fair to explore some of the 350 societies on offer and maybe to enjoy a few of the many performances taking place throughout the day. Jemma appeared carefree, all last night's minor trauma put to the back of her mind. The first person they bumped into was Ben looking very much worse for wear.

"I'll never learn will I?"

"You look like shit Ben." Jemma smiled, herself understanding what it felt like the morning after a night of drinking too much.

"Thanks for that Jemma. What are you girls into, sports fair on Friday and then Freshers fair next week, lot's of giveaways then, loads of societies wanting you to join. Today's really about tickling your taste buds although there are some interesting performances going on level 2."

In some ways Sam resented Ben setting himself up as their unofficial guide. She might have preferred it if she and Jemma had done the exploring and investigating on their own but then he was only being kind wasn't he or was he?

"Got your tickets for the Freshers UV Neon Rave yet? Confetti Showers on show girls, mustn't miss that." They agreed with him about that and bought tickets right there and then. Truth was they were a bit late and missed a lot of the events on show although they did catch the Chinese Classical Dance performance. Then as they came down stairs to get some food a small rather dark skinned girl came up to them grinning all over her face.

"How's it going then. I'm just down the corridor from you two, seen you around. I'm Sophie." She held out a brown hand which they all took turns in shaking. "See you've got tickets for the bash." And that was how the duo of girls became a trio.

The group moved on to the students' bar in need of refreshment. Ben bought them a round of drinks, asking Sam if she would mind helping him carry them back to the table where the other two girls had established themselves. His real reason for asking for Sam's help however was to get her on her own for a bit so he could ask her round to the house he shared with three other students for a meal.

"One of my house-mates is a girl," he added thinking that might make the decision that much easier.

"I don't know Ben. You're a nice guy and all that but it's early days and I don't want to desert Jemma." When he looked crest-fallen she quickly added, "Plenty of time. Let me get more settled in before I go visiting."

Chapter 3

Sam's first two weeks at university were certainly hectic ones. She'd signed up for hockey at the Sports Fair despite being warned that the difference in standard between schoolgirl hockey and what was expected at college was wider than might have been expected. Then at the activities fair she thought she'd see what the performing arts society was all about. Ben had continued on the scene and she had gone out with him to a local pub on a couple of occasions, but she made it absolutely clear that she wasn't looking for a boyfriend at this stage in her life. Her two friends Jemma and Sophie had signed up to one or two things but Jemma said that her part time job would use up most of her spare time so she wouldn't have much left for sports or societies. Sophie on the other hand was very into netball. She had played for the school team although again she was worried that her school level of skills might not match up to what was required at university.

Now Monday morning, the skies dark overhead, it seemed to Sam that the realities of life at university had arrived with a bang. Lectures started today and while she was eager to get started on her course it seemed on that Monday morning that everything had now changed. Even Ben would have to leave her alone for a while as he started work on his second year studies. Neither Jemma nor

Sophie were taking the same course as Sam so she was about to meet some new students, friends perhaps. She gathered her notebooks and set off for the lecture hall with a faint air of trepidation although she wasn't sure why. After all this is what she'd come to college for wasn't it? As she crossed the campus it came on to rain so she broke into a run to complete her journey to the lecture hall arriving out of breath and a trifle dishevelled.

There were several students there already eager to get started. Still out of breath she took a seat near the rear of the hall without really noticing the people she was sitting next to. One was a girl who at once introduced herself as Rebecca and on the other side a boy who took his time before turning to her with a slowly emerging smile. "And I'm Chistopher Malpas, sometimes called Kit." Sam liked the guy on sight, liked his easy manner, liked the way he appeared to offer friendship perhaps yet at the same time didn't seem to care whether the offer was accepted or not.

The lecturer came in at that point and things kicked off with the usual rather bland introduction. What is Psychology? What types of psychology are there? What are its uses and what impact does it have? Half way through that first session Kit switched that slow smile again. "Don't worry I'm sure it will get more interesting as the term goes on."

It seemed quite natural that her new friend should suggest they grab something to eat after the rigours of their first lecture. It was still raining when they came out of the hall so they ran across the campus to the Arts Tower Café where Kit said they could get a couple of jacket potatoes and a cup of coffee. He appeared to know his way round and the campus already. They arrived rather wet and dishevelled laughing at each other's appearance. There was no doubt about it Sam liked this Kit even after only their very brief acquaintance although she put such thoughts to the back of her mind for the time being. She was here to work not to get involved with boys. As if as a reminder her cell phone went off at this point. When she saw it was Maggie, her mum, calling she took the call and dealt with the anxious parent with a few appropriate clichés.

"What made you go for Psychology then?" They were seated at a table, baked potatoes in front of them when Kit asked the question.

Sam gave a little shrug of her shoulders. "Default really. I was pretty desperate to get away to Uni and it was either that or geography and there seemed more scope in the psychology option." She was being quite honest but put like that it did sound rather feeble.

It must have been half an hour later when her new friend exclaimed, "Oh my God is that the time? I've got a squash court booked, must fly. Sorry to leave like this but don't want to let Freddie down. See you around."

And he was gone. Sam was surprised at her own reaction, at her own feelings. She hadn't wanted him to go yet. She would have liked to find out more about Cristopher Malpas although she wasn't sure why. Sam got up ready to leave the café when a familiar face appeared.

"So that's where you've been hiding." Ben grinned like a Cheshire cat that had just found the cream he'd been looking for. How'd it go, first lecture and all that stuff?"

Sam smiled back. He was a nice boy and had done his best to introduce her to life on the campus. Then those thoughts about not wanting a relationship swept back into her mind although somewhat confused now after her meeting with Kit. Anyway right now she didn't really want to join up with Ben no matter how helpful he'd been.

"Can I get you another of those?" Ben nodded towards the can of coke lying on the table.

"No thanks Ben, I'm off back to my room to read through this morning's notes."

The boy looked disappointed. "Going to be in the students'bar this evening?"

"Wouldn't be surprised." She offered another friendly smile. The two of them left the café together and walked in the direction of the halls of residence where Sam said goodbye. Instead of going to her own room she knocked at Jemma's door feeling like a girly chat, one which might have involved boys. Sophie was already there drinking coffee. For some reason Sam felt disappointed by her presence. The truth was that she was being utterly selfish yet she couldn't help feeling that she'd found Jemma first and now this late- comer was getting in on her act as it were. At once she put aside her spoilt little girl thoughts and got down to asking the other two how their first day's lectures had gone. All the time while the three girls were light-heartedly talking about lectures Sam was longing to tell Jemma about her meeting with Kit Malpas yet for some reason she didn't want to do so while Sophie was there.

It was later that day, when Sam was well clear of her earlier sulky mood, that Sam at last managed to get Jemma on her own. They were on their way to the student union bar when she told her friend about Kit. "You're looking a bit flushed Sam. He must have made an impression."

"Well," Sam hesitated, "he did seem rather nice and not pushy like dear old Ben."

"Made arrangements to see him again then sweety?"

"No nothing like that. Just thought I'd mention him that's all. Nice to meet new people don't you think?"

"Oh I do, I really do." Jemma grinned widely putting an arm round Sam's shoulders as they continued their leisurely walk towards the bar.

Not unexpectedly the first person they came across once inside the teeming room was Ben, eager as usual to get the first round of drinks. "Where's young Sophie then," he asked.

"She's gone into town with her new friend."

Whether he'd been looking out for her or not didn't really matter, he was there, as large as life. Sam introduced Kit to the others and got a frown from Ben for her trouble. Sam was well aware that Ben regarded Kit as an intruder on his patch while she was keen to learn more about the young man she'd met for the first time only a few hours ago. Was she changing her mind about no boyfriends while at college, no serious ones anyway? At that point in time she didn't think in those terms. Her thoughts were confined to exploration of a mild friendship. One in which she had no specific intentions at all, yet when her new friend suddenly and openly turned to her and asked if she fancied a trip to one of the city pubs one evening she smilingly agreed. They fixed up the following evening for what had now to be considered a date. She could tell Ben was furious and wasn't really surprised when short time afterwards he made the excuse of having to complete an essay, abruptly leaving the group without finishing his beer.

"You've done it now Sam," Jemma grinned at her friend. "Anyway I'm off too so I'll leave you two to get to know each other."

Left alone Kit and Sam were at first at a loss of what to say to one another. "Did I put my foot in it with that Ben chap?"

"No of course not. Ben's a good chap but he's not my boyfriend or anything like that."

Almost despite herself Sam felt a growing sense of attraction towards this rather solemn young man. There was something reliable about him, something that told you he would never let you down. But having said that were those feelings Sam felt inside her in any way amorous in the normal boy/girl sense. She wasn't sure. Of one thing she was sure and that was she was looking forward to the next day and their outing to the City.

When she got back to her room she found her mood was vibrant. She didn't feel at all tired, she felt so alive that it came over as a restlessness that she couldn't shake off so she slipped next door to talk to Jemma who seemed to recognise that very vibrancy she had felt herself a few moments earlier.

"My God what has that boy done to you? You look like the cat that got the cream."

It's true that Sam's eyes were shining although that could be put down to the beers she'd put away earlier in the evening. Jemma didn't think so.

"Don't be daft. It's just that I'm enjoying life at college."

"Oh yes," said with raised eyebrows and pursed lips. "And what about this Kit chap. You saying he's got nothing to do with your euphoric state. All this sparkle has nothing to do with that invitation to go out to the pub tomorrow?"

Sam grinned. "He's nice that's all. No harm in going out for a drink with a nice boy is there?"

"Absolutely none sweety. What about a coffee to bring you back down to earth?" She was grinning all over her face as she hugged Sam in a spontaneous embrace. I'm looking forward to an update after tomorrow's little outing.

The two girls sat chatting and drinking coffee into the early hours until Jemma shooed her friend out saying she needed her sleep if she was to be at her best for her assignation with Kit the next day.

In the morning there was a meeting before the promised outing to the pub which Sam had now decided to classify as a date, because both she and Kit attended the same lecture. She arrived late and took the nearest seat available rather than finding one next to Kit. He smiled over at her and gave a little wave of his hand to which she offered a shy response. When the teaching finished they naturally came together.

"You still on for tonight?" When she nodded, he continued, "Great, see you at the entrance to the campus in my old Riley at about half seven. Got to go now to meet up with my tutor for the first time. Wish me luck." And before she could think of much to say he was off leaving Sam wondering what to do. She didn't have long to wonder because Ben strolled up.

"Your new boyfriend deserted you then?"

"Hello Ben. He's not my boyfriend, we just happened to be taking the same course that's all, not that it's any of your business anyway."

Ben took another tack suggesting that they go for a quick bite to the Arts Tower Café to which she smilingly agreed. Sam was a nice natured girl with absolutely no wish to hurt Ben's feelings yet at the same time she didn't want him to get any wrong ideas.

They sat there eating their hotdogs and drinking beer just like two old friends. Ben must have felt comfortable with the situation because he suddenly looked across the table. "So if that guy's not your boyfriend what about you and me going out one evening?"

"Look Ben you've been very helpful settling me into college life but really I'm not looking for any kind of relationship just now. My date, if that's what it is, with Kit is because we have our studies in common and we might be useful to each other." My God how feeble that sounded she thought as soon as the words were out of her mouth.

Ben sighed. "If you say so." And then sulked for the rest of their lunch, hardly saying another word.

That evening the weather had turned colder. Sam waiting at the edge of the campus was glad she put on a jacket and a silk scarf. Right on time an old Riley pulled up and she recognised Kit's face leaning out of the car window. What did surprise her was that there appeared to be another passenger already in the car. "Sorry about this Sam but this reprobate is my brother Lionel. I would normally have told him to get lost but he turned up out of the blue. He's only go, two days left of his leave so I could hardly not include him in our outing – hope you don't mind."

Sam did mind of course. She had wanted the evening to be a getting-to-know-you evening; with that damn brother there that wasn't going to happen. "No of course not, pleased to meet you Lionel."

It transpired that Lionel was in the army and the conversation, not unnaturally, focussed to a large extent on his recent experiences in Afghanistan where he had served as helicopter pilot with plenty of stories to tell. It turned out to be a pleasant enough evening but not the sort that Sam has hoped for. When the brothers dropped her off back at the campus she was left with a vague feeling of disappointment which was still with her when she got back to her room. She hadn't found out anything about

31

Christopher Malpas and while the attraction was still there she wondered whether her feelings had outpaced the circumstances which in fact only amounted to a couple of meetings, very much arms-length meetings at that.

Sam should have been doing some reading as specified by the lecturer, but wasn't in the mood so she went to bed instead to spend a restless night haunted by dreams of getting lost in a forest in which she spent what seemed like hours trying to find a way out of the thick undergrowth. In the morning she woke with a sense that something wasn't quite right which left her uneasy.

With some feeling of resignation she collected herself together, made coffee before trying to catch up with some of the reading she should have done yesterday. By the time she was due in the lecture hall she was feeling better although she was still unsure of how she would react if she happened to meet Kit which was highly likely as he would be attending the lecture that day.

She was early for once and was just settling into her seat when the object of quite a lot of her recent thinking dropped in beside her. "Hi Sam. Look I'm really sorry about last night. You must have been bored out of your socks with Lionel going on about the bloody army, but I didn't know he was coming and he was only here for one night so I could hardly ignore him, could I?" It all came out in a rush accompanied by a look which could be regarded as contrition. Whatever it was it made Sam feel better.

"Not to worry. It was very interesting and I liked your brother."

"Anyway we must do it again and this time without the military commentary."

Sam was pleased. She had decided that her time in college was to be spent in studying yet this boy intrigued her and she felt herself urging him on to define the half suggestion for another meeting that he'd just come out with. She didn't have long to wait.

"How about tonight. Shall we meet up in the students bar say about eightish?"

That was why Sam was sipping a pint of beer that evening her eyes searching the thronging mass to locate the illusive Christopher Malpas. Time went by. Ben came over to chat but drifted away when she told him she was meeting up with Kit. She saw Jemma on the other side of the room chatting to a fair-haired boy and they exchanged waves but still no Kit. Her pint glass was nearly empty when she finally decided she'd been stood up. She was disappointed and a bit cross. In a fit of pique she decided she'd go back to her room and do some work. Five minutes after she'd sat down at her desk there was a knock on her door. When she opened it there was a rueful looking young man pulling a face and raising his arms in supplication.

"Sam what can I say. I seem to be spending our time together apologising." Part of his apology was to lean forward to kiss her cheek which in an instance changed Sam's mood from one of recrimination to one of mild excitement. He went on to explain that his mother, a widow, had rung him worried about something to do with her benefits.

"She's always been bothered about anything she regards as officialdom. She seems to think they must be right because they are who they are. With Lionel in the army and me here at college she feels vulnerable I suppose."

Sam wondered whether she should ask when Kit's dad had died but then decided it was too early for that and went back to making the coffee. "Not to worry – families eh?" That brought her back to thinking about her own, what she regarded as over-protective, parents. To make her visitor feel more relaxed she jokingly told him about Maggie and Trylon and their close parenting despite and feeling slightly guilty about her minor betrayal.

It was good that a youngster should care about his mother and it reinforced her view that he was someone who wouldn't let you down, not that there was anything to let her down about just yet. Sam kept glancing across at her visitor who was sitting in the only chair in the room while she perched on the bed. She was pleased to see him gradually relaxing as he sipped his coffee.

"Apart from your studies and your squash what else are you involved in?"

Kit looked faintly embarrassed. "Well I did put down for performing arts but I haven't been to any sessions as yet and I'm not sure I will."

Sam laughed. "So did I and I haven't followed it up either. Perhaps we can go to a session together."

After that they chatted on into the night apparently enjoying each other's company without the need for anything too close. There was something very much unspoken in the air during all the time they were chatting, something to do with sex, but so far undefined. It needed one of them to make a move if, and it was a big if, anything was going to happen that evening. Eventually Kit said he'd better go and get some sleep. As he got up from the chair and moved towards the door there was a slight frown on his face as though he was trying to remember something he'd forgotten. At the door he stopped, turned, and in a swift move that took Sam, who had moved over to say goodbye, completely by surprise, he pulled her into his arms and kissed her in a way that left no doubt about his desires towards her. Then just as suddenly he broke away to stand on the threshold looking slightly embarrassed.

Sam smiled to show what she felt about the kiss and would have been very happy to engage in more of them, but it appeared that Kit had decided that was enough for that evening. Sam was used to boys in those circumstances trying to go as far as she would let them, not this boy though. He was going to move at his own pace he seemed to be saying. Sam could take it or leave it. It was very early days and Sam was happy to let this serious young man lead the dance.

When he'd gone she had to admit to a feeling of disappointment. She had been aroused by the kiss and had wanted and expected things to go further, but then she was philosophical about it. After all she was the one who had promised herself she wouldn't be diverted by relationships while she was at college. As she undressed for bed sensuality was still on her and she slipped beneath the duvet naked and unusually for her moved her hands tantalisingly over her body while imagining what it would be like if her recent visitor was doing the caressing.

She was still in a state of semi-euphoria when she woke next day, going next door ostensibly to see how Jemma was doing but actually to give vent to her feeling about Christopher Malpas. She had to tell someone how she felt about him or she'd burst. A bleary-eyed Jemma opened her door and let her excited friend into the room. Before she could get a word out Jemma was gabbling away about the boy she'd met in the pub where she had her part-time job as a barmaid. "He's gorgeous I tell you Sam, you'll love him when you meet him."

That rather took the wind out of Sam's sails but being the kind-natured girl she was, she let Jemma continue her spiel about the latest boy in her life until finally she paused for breath. "What about your guy Sam? You had a date last night, didn't you?"

Somehow in the face of Jemma's enthusiastic tirade her own encounter last night paled in significance. "Yes went well. I like him, came back for coffee and........"

Jemma laughed "And what?"

"Not what you're thinking anyway."

Their mutual love lives were put on hold at that point when they were joined by Sophie who rather disappointingly had nothing to report of a romantic nature. The three of them drank coffee before going their separate ways to attend the day's lectures.

When Sam arrived at the lecture hall she decided to play it cool. Kit excited her and she badly wanted to find out more about him, yet at the same time she wasn't going to be running after any boy no matter how nice he seemed. She needn't have worried because barely had she settled in the seat when along came the object of her thoughts to ask the girl sitting next to her if she would move up to let him take the seat next to her. It was a Friday and the question of how to spend the coming weekend was something she expected they would be discussing. She was right but not quite in the way she'd expected. During a break when there was a change of lecturer Kit asked her what she had planned for the weekend. When she shrugged Kit looked a trifle uneasy.

"Look Sam. I want to spend time with you but I promised I'd pop over and see my mum some time on Saturday. Why don't you come with me? She only lives in Scunthorpe, only take a few minutes in the car."

Meet his mother! No that was moving far too fast for Sam. "No Kit, you go off and see you mum, we can meet up later."

He looked dejected at her refusal. "It would give you chance to see a bit of Yorkshire. I'm sure she'd love to meet you."

He looked so disappointed Sam hadn't the heart to turn his invitation down even though she thought meeting Kit's mother might imply rather more than she wanted it to at this stage. After all they'd only met a few times, exchanged one kiss. Meeting Mrs. Malpas might be taken to mean she was being given the once over to be a future member of Kit's family.

She sighed. "OK then Kit, but just a brief visit, no staying over-night or anything."

That was why on Saturday morning Sam was sitting in the draughty seat of an old Riley speeding along a Yorkshire road towards what she didn't know. She hadn't wanted this because it seemed to suggest something that wasn't yet there if it ever would be. She liked Kit, wanted to continue their friendship, but for Sam these things took time. Perhaps that reticence came from her dad, Trylon, who with Maggie had brought her up in a household where everything was carefully considered before any action was taken. Whatever it was Sam was by that upbringing and indeed her very nature a cautious girl.

When they arrived at Mrs's Malpas's home Sam was relieved to find, not an upmarket town house, but a modest cottage on the outskirts of Scunthorpe, a cottage which revealed its owner as a keen gardener. In fact the lady in question was there in the garden doing some autumn clearing up the summer debris when they pulled into the drive. The lady was wearing an old pair of jeans and a bulky old sweater that had once been white but now more grey than white. As they drew to a halt the gardener threw her gloves and her secateurs into a wheelbarrow before advancing to welcome the newcomers, a broad smile across her face. As she hugged her son in a close embrace, she looked quizzically over his shoulder to catch Sam's eye. Then releasing her son she took a stride towards Sam and without hesitation planted a kiss on her cheek.

"So you're Samantha then? You certainly live up to my son's description of you as pretty my dear."

Her smile appeared to Sam to be warm and genuine. She knew mothers and their prospective daughters-in-law could sometimes be at odds with regard to the male in the picture, but apparently not with this lady. She seemed to accept Sam as a friend of her son's without conditions and with no regard to a future possible relationship. The afternoon passed pleasantly enough with tea and questions. It turned out that the redoubtable Mrs. Malpas was quite a successful author of children's stories She played down her successful career, quickly changing the subject to Sam and what *she* wanted to do with her life then onto Sam's family and her life before arriving at Sheffield University. She seemed to quite understand the young girl's delight with college life so far.

"You know Sam you should enjoy your time at Uni but never forget your mum and dad. They brought you up according to their own mores and while you might see your childhood as perhaps restrictive, they did a good job in giving you a start in life, I'm sure."

It was then that Sam realised that what she had been saying about her early years at home had been a mild betrayal of Trylon and Maggie.

"Yes, I do know that Mrs Malpas. If I appeared ungrateful, then I was at fault. In fact I love them both dearly."

"Of course you do dear. I wasn't trying to imply otherwise and by the way please call me Edith. I really think we're going to be friends." She passed over the plate on which rested a sponge cake she'd baked herself. Sam smiling at her own greed took another slice which seemed to seal their rapport.

Towards evening Kit began to show signs of restlessness so Sam wasn't surprised when she heard him say that they had to be going, although as far as she knew there was no reason at all for them to leave. It was Kit's home, his visit, so she went along with the suggestion that they had to leave without demur.

In the car on the way back to Sheffield Sam asked, "Why the rush. I liked your mum and liked chatting to her. Bit mean, rushing off like that."

Kit turned towards her raising his eyebrows in a quizzical look. "It was only a duty call. My mother is quite happy with her own company and her bridge mates I can assure you."

He didn't see the small frown that passed across Sam's face but might have sensed that she was not entirely happy with his reply. Anyway that was all soon forgotten when the subject of the Sheffield University Performing Arts Society came up. They had both expressed interest and were due to attend a special meeting for newcomers the following evening.

"What made you go for that Kit?"

He laughed. "Tell you the truth, I couldn't think what to go for and I thought that might have some mileage in it. Not that I've ever done any acting in my life but there you are, just a whim."

Their relaxed conversation came to an abrupt halt when, out of the blue, Kit braked to a stop in a field entrance, turned to her with what appeared to be a worried look before moving over to kiss her, at first slowly and gently but then with mounting passion. There's no doubt that had not the inside of the Morgan been so cramped

39

those kisses might have led on to unrestrained sex. As it was the intimacy of their caresses, the exploration of eager hands, set the seal on a relationship emphatically sexual. All those resolutions about college being for hard work and dedicated study, paled in the face of this new obsession that had overtaken Sam.

Back on the campus Kit went away to park the car before coming back to Sam's room where she had promised him a cup of coffee. What he got, and what they both expected, was a naked session on Sam's bed culminating in a way both said afterwards they'd never experienced before. There was no mistake. Sam had a boyfriend. She had a lover and everything else paled into insignificance.

Chapter 4

It was two days later when Sam and Kit went together to the introductory session of SUPAS. They were still full of each other, yet this foray into the unknowns of the performing arts was still exciting. There was quite a crowd and Ross Telliman, the main speaker, spent the first part of his introductory talk going over housekeeping matters and outlining the work that the second and third year students had already started on. The two newcomers pricked up their ears when it came to the latest SUPAS plans. They were going to put on Baby Doll by Tennessee Williams. Ross handed round a synopsis of the play and then to those who still appeared to be interested he offered short scripts for the various parts that prospective actors could use at their auditions. Both Sam and Kit took both sheets of paper although neither of them had made any decisions about how far they wanted to get involved.

"Typical Tennessee Williams." The lovers were back in Sam's room drinking coffee. "And as far as I can see there are only three parts that matter so the chances of our being asked to get involved are very slight indeed. I'm not really into that decadent deep South stuff anyway. What do you think Sam?"

"You're probably right Kit although we could possibly get involved in some of the 'behind the scenes' work."

The boy laughed and reached out to take her in his arms. "To hell with SUPAS. I'm more interested in our own personal bit of theatre."

"Hold on a minute Kit. I hate to be a killjoy but my period came on this morning and well, you know."

Her words stopped Kit in his tracks. It was as though he'd been clubbed with something heavy. "I could take the tampon out if you're desperate." She spoke without thinking; then seeing Kit's face she realised how much she'd embarrassed her lover.

His arms fell away from her, his face red with embarrassment. "That's more information than I need," he mouthed apologetically.

Sam laughed. "Why do boys get so embarrassed when the subject of menstruation crops up? All us females suffer from the curse you know so if you're looking for a girl without that problem I reckon you'll be disappointed.

Desperately trying to recover his composure Kit shook his head. "No, sorry sweetie, you just took me by surprise that's all. Nothing to worry about is it?"

"Not for you mate." She laughed again.

The exchange had been embarrassing, at least for Kit, but at the same time it introduced a degree of intimacy that augured well for their future relationship. In the early days of a male/female relationship sex usually came high on the agenda. Now on that particular evening the enticement of sexual intimacy had been put on the back-burner leaving a passionate young couple each unsure about their next moves.

Kit, eager to make up for his earlier clumsiness, tried to encircle Sam in his arms and although she submitted happily to his embrace the spark had gone out at least for that particular evening. She smiled at him with a degree of understanding he probably didn't deserve. "How about we try the Writers' Club. There's a meeting tomorrow and I've always wanted to try my hand at writing a novel."

Kit, pleased to be on to a nice neutral subject readily agreed, and after some tender goodnight kissing they called it a day. When Kit left, Sam felt lonely but only for a moment. She liked the guy very much and smart girl that she was realised that everyone came with their own particular foibles, that if you loved someone you loved that person warts and all. Once her mind set had adjusted to that maxim she felt fine again and went to bed in a happy frame of mind.

In the morning Sam didn't feel too well. She often suffered from mild stomach cramps during her period so it wasn't unexpected. She didn't have time to dwell on it anyway because a knock on the door announced the arrival of Jemma brimming over with news of the boy she'd met during her work as a barmaid in the city pub. What had started up as a casual date now appeared to be morphing into something more serious. Her enthusiastic description of all that was great about Tommy Foreman was cut short by the arrival of Sophie with her own boyfriend news. Ben had at last had some success in his search for love. A slightly sheepish Sophy explained that she'd agreed to give him a chance and a date had been arranged for that evening. Sam remained quiet amongst all the girlish chatter although inside she felt confident about her thing with Christopher Malpas. Had she felt more up to the mark she might have done some of her own boasting. As it was she made them all coffee and instead listened to her friends tales of love.

But she wasn't to be allowed her quiet introspection for long. "And what about you Sam? You've been very subdued this morning, got your monthlies or what?"

Sam sighed. "Well if you must know I have, but I can tell you for nothing that there's nothing amiss with my lovelife."

"Oh yes and have you done the deed yet?" There were no secrets to be kept from the exuberant Jemma.

Despite herself, Sam's frown was accompanied by cheeks turning a pale shade of pink. "Why don't you mind your own business Jemma, concentrate on your own sex life and leave me to pursue mine." Just for a moment she was really angry but then she quickly understood there was no malice in her good-natured friend with her mischievous comments.

Jemma took no notice except to say, "Well we know the answer to that one anyway I think."

Sophie amused by the interplay between her two friends changed the subject. "Have you two got tickets for the Freshers UV Neon Rave on Saturday?" Sam and Jemma looked blank. "Just as well I've got a couple of spares then," she smiled, enjoying her moment of control. Sam's immediate thought was for Kit. There was no way she was going raving without her boyfriend was there? Anyway before that she and Kit were already lined up to attend the first meeting of the writers club and that was the very next day.

When the two young lovers arrived at the meeting room the next day it was crowded with enthusiasts of the written word. Samuel Dodgeson who appeared to be the man in charge, banged his fist on the table to gain their attention.

"Look guys it's great to see so many budding writers here tonight but hell I think we're swamped. If you're up for it I think the only way out is for us to split into two or three groups with perhaps some coming together at the end of term or the end of year. There are a couple of third year members who I'm sure would love to facilitate a couple of groups and I'll take the other one." He glanced sideways at two of the students sitting with him at the table, one male, one female. You could almost hear the sighs although there were also shrugs of the shoulders. "Right thanks guys. This is Emily Horncastle and this handsome chap is Roger Fairweather. There are rooms next door so I suggest existing members spread themselves into the three groups with newcomer s joining in so we get approximately equal numbers in the three groups."

Sam and Kit decided to join Emily's group and followed her out into the next room like a flock of school kids following their teacher. A confident Emily took charge, explaining how things had worked in previous years and asking for each person there to give a rundown on why they wanted to join the writers club and what they had achieved so far by way of writing. As could be imagined this took some time. When they'd all had their moments in the limelight Emily suggested they pick a prompt and each write a short piece based on that ready for the next meeting. Someone came up with 'The Reunion' so it was agreed on that as the subject for the next time they met in a week's time.

As they left the building on the way back to Sam's room Kit put his arm round her shoulder. "How would you fancy a weekend away sweetie?"

"I've told you before I hate being called that. Anyway what's all this about a weekend away?"

My mum's off to visit her sister in Durham so there's an empty cottage we can use as a love nest for a whole two days. What do you think?"

What Sam did think was not for airing just then but she did look her boyfriend straight in the eye and muttered, "Maybe."

"What do you mean 'maybe'. It's a glorious chance to spend a weekend in glorious debauchery. I thought you'd jump at the idea."

She sighed. "Taking things for granted as usual Christopher. The truth is I haven't even started on that essay that has to in for next Tuesday." She was teasing of course. Kit shook his head and frowned.

"Please yourself Sam. It seemed like a good opportunity to me."

"A good opportunity for you to get your leg over you mean. There is a life beyond sex you know and writing essays is part of that."

Sam knew all along that the suggested weekend to be spent in her boyfriend's family home *would* take place but the lad had to work for it.

When they got back to Sam's room she shooed him out saying she had work to do but that she'd let him know about that weekend tomorrow. Left alone Sam found herself in an introspective mood. She liked Kit but was he getting too serious? She had promised her mum and dad in all seriousness that she would make the most of her time at college and in their eyes that meant working to get a good degree and here she was up to her eyes in a relationship which might just take her mind off her studies. She sighed to herself, pursed her lips and reaffirmed in her mind that promise to her parents.

She had been there before when Kit had taken her to meet his mum but this was different. A house all to themselves. The first thing Kit did was to show her round the family home including his own room which was little changed from what it had been when he was a schoolboy.

He was a trifle embarrassed by why might be considered the immaturity of the room's contents with posters on the wall of outdated bands and a collection of Corgi cars that he laughingly said he was going to donate to the local charity shop. Having Sam in his room must have stirred some adolescent phantasies because, after his bout of self-mockery, he suddenly grabbed her, kissed her with savage intensity pushing her back onto the bed. Sam made a show of resistance, but she too felt the sexy excitement of making love in a schoolboy's bedroom and quickly joined in with enthusiasm.

It was after that sudden bout of exuberant love-making that Sam began to think again about what she was doing in this thing with Kit. While he dozed by her side on the small bed in that schoolboy's bedroom she worried. She had come to college to work not to get tangled in some love affair no matter how cute her lover might be. He was a good-looking guy, nice natured, but hell she was only nineteen and the rest of her life lay before her like the map of exciting new territory yet to be explored. Did she want to go through her college years joined at the hip to a bloke no matter how nice he was? When Kit lifted his head, opened his eyes, and asked if she would like a cup of tea, she banished those serious thoughts for consideration at another time. In the meantime a weekend of relaxed debauchery was not to be sneezed at if that was the right metaphor.

Kit turned out to be a reasonable cook and as they sat in front of the fire forking up their spaghetti strands they were just two good mates enjoying each other's company. Mind you the chianti which Kit had borrowed from his mum's wine rack didn't go amiss. Later they watched a video of a Ken Loach film 'I'm Sorry We Missed You'. Sam had known her boyfriend was socially minded but if that was the sort of thing he was into he could count her out.

"My God Kit do you call that entertainment. If I want a harrowing experience I'll read the newspapers thank you."

"Yes it was certainly emotional, yet you know extreme as it was it does represent something of life's reality for a section of our community. We middle class guys and dolls are largely sheltered from those realities you know."

"Look Kit I'm sure you're sincere but not tonight if you don't mind. I'm serious. If you don't lighten up I'm off to catch the last bus back to college and you can stay and make yourself miserable all on your own."

He sighed. "I'm sorry Sam but you have to admit that Loach's films do get under your skin."

"Probably but I'm not in the mood. Put some damn music on and pour me another glass of that chianti." The wine was all gone but Kit did find a CD of Ariana Grande which helped to reset the mood of the evening. "You want dry ginger with this?" he asked holding out a tumbler of amber liquid.

"Better had. I don't usually drink whisky. You're not trying to get me into bed are you Christopher Malpas?"

"Wouldn't dream of it my sweet."

That changed mood was now firmly established and they sat arm in arm in front of the dying embers listening to the music and enjoying just being together.

Later, despite some protestation from Sam, they slept in his mother's double bed. 'Slept' was perhaps a very distant euphemism for what went on in that bed. All Sam's thoughts about her relationship with the boy were put to one side. She loved the feel of that beautiful boyish body and loved the feel of his hands exploring every nook and cranny of her own body. Whatever her real feelings were for Christopher Malpas, one thing was for sure, she loved having sex with him and that night that was all that mattered. There wasn't much talking but what there was had nothing to do with the woes of what Kit might have described as the underclass of the United Kingdom.

It was a great weekend. They went to see Adrian Lyne's version of Nobokov's Lolita in Sheffield on Saturday, lunch at the Mason's Arms on Sunday. A weekend at the end of which Sam felt her doubts about Christopher had evaporated. She was in love with the boy and while her commitment to study was still strong it would have to progress along with that love that kept her in a constant state of inner euphoria, a lovely sweet intoxication of the mind that had overtaken her every waking moment.

Chapter 5

Shock wasn't a strong enough word for Sam's feelings. Her periods had always been regular and even when the expected arrival of the one due was late, she was only slightly anxious rather than worried. The days went by. She took a pregnancy test which proved positive, she went to see the campus nurse who made an appointment with the doctor, she went to see her personal tutor, and finally she told Kit. Up to this point she still hadn't mentioned anything to Maggie or Trylon. The day that happened would be a traumatic event in its own right.

"Pregnant, fucking hell? How can you be pregnant? Pills and all that stuff." His face was a mask, a grim mask of not wanting to believe what he was hearing. He slumped back in his chair, ran his hands through his hair, and closed his eyes.

"Is that all you can say Christopher? You might not like it but I repeat I'm pregnant and you are the prospective father."

"Father? What do you mean father? You're surely not thinking of having this baby, are you?"

The tears were already running down Sam's cheeks. What she needed just then was comforting and understanding. What she got was disbelief and anger. This was a Christopher Malpas she didn't recognise. A look on his face she'd never seen before. Her misery deepened with every passing moment.

Then as though something had clicked in his brain the shocked young man dragged himself to his feet and came over to where Sam was sitting on her bed. "I'm sorry love but you must understand you quite took the wind out of my sails. Of course I'll accept my responsibilities but we have two lives to consider here, two educations and……." His attempt to take her in his arms was shrugged away angrily by Sam.

"Weighing it all up are you Kit? I've known about this for days now, worried myself sick, needed some support, perhaps even some love or is that too much to ask?"

He sighed, shook his head and tried again to put his arms round her. "You're right sweetheart I'm a callous sod and I'm sorry, but hell this is one great problem we have between us." This time she succumbed to his embrace, nestling against his chest and sobbing great sobs of misery while he stroked her hair and wondered what he should say next. He didn't want to become a father when he was just starting out on his studies yet he had to be very careful what he said from now on. This was one very upset girl and the situation needed all the tact he possessed. His thoughts were all about how they could rid themselves of this problem baby while he quickly realised that Sam's views were far more complicated and involved things like the morality of abortion and her own attitude towards the new life growing in her womb.

The two of them stayed like that entwined in apparent affection, yet each with their own turbulent thoughts. Eventually they slipped beneath the duvet and slept for what was left of the night but, that night, only slept. Anything else was out of the question for now with

Sam's pregnancy looming over them like a dark cloud. The wonderfulness of an impending birth wasn't something that came quickly to mind during that long night, certainly not for Christopher Malpas anyway.

In the morning Christopher woke to an empty bed. He yawned, stretched, reluctant to emerge into the cold light of day and what he recognised as one hell of a problem. That was going to need all his tact and goodwill, even love maybe.

"Come on Kit we've got a lecture this morning." Even in his current state of mind the sight of a radiant Sam with a towel round her was enough to stir his libido.

"I could think of other things I'd prefer to do," he joked.

"Yes, well, I think we know where that leads don't we." She was stern that morning although not in any accusing manner. After all this so called problem they had was a joint thing. As she got dressed she said, half to herself, "I wonder what my mum will say when she finds out I'm up the duff."

The day passed like most of the days without major incident. Sam was back in her room, her mood one of deep concern about the small thing growing inexorably inside her. She needed to talk to someone about her condition, someone other than Kit or her tutor. Someone who loved her and understood how she thought. She couldn't talk to her mum without involving Trylon, and anyway she needed some internal armour before she presented her parents with her pregnancy bombshell. There was only one person in the world who fitted that bill, her grandmother Grace. Yes she decided she would go and see her gran, talk things through with the wise old thing.

In the evening as expected Kit came round, a very serious young man that evening and while he did offer some comfort and made an attempt to discuss their mutual predicament he was much too personally involved to be of much use to Sam.

"Tell you what Kit, I'm going to see my grandmother in Derby, have a chat with her."

The boy shrugged failing to see what good that would do. Then realising his insensitivity he offered. "OK love, I'll drive you there if you like."

"No I think it's best I go on my own."

He shrugged again. "I was only trying to help."

Sam had been rapidly considering her options which included changing her mind. "Well you could Kit as long as you don't mind dropping me off and picking me up from my gran's later."

Christopher did drive Sam to Derby. During the journey the atmosphere in the car was strained to say the least. The driver was unclear about what this visit was all about. Sam had made it clear he wasn't invited to meet her grandmother so he wasn't likely to unless Sam herself spilled whatever beans there were.

Sam watched the Riley drive away before she rang the front door bell of Grace's small but neat town house. Sam had given Grace no warning of her visit so the old lady let out a cry of surprise when she opened the door to find her granddaughter standing on the step. "Oh my God Samantha, you made my heart stop. What are you doing here and how did you get here? It's a long way from Sheffield, chuck."

"Aren't you glad to see me then gran?"

"Course I am lovey, but you startled me that's all. Come and sit down I'll make us a cup of tea and then you can give me your news."

Grace was what you might call scraggy, but Sam knew only too well beneath that bag of bones was a strong lively no nonsense personality that would give and take with the best of them. She followed her grandmother into the kitchen and watched her fuss around finding mugs and rooting out a tin from the cupboard which she promised contained a cherry cake still fresh enough to eat. When all was prepared to her satisfaction they sat down at the kitchen table.

"Right, now sweetheart you going to tell me what this about or what?. You don't come all this way unless you're in some sort of trouble. Grace was looking very directly at her young visitor waiting for a response.

While Sam took a sip of tea from her mug she focused on the far kitchen wall rather than on her grandmother's hard stare. She wasn't sure where to start and even then how she would explain why she was there once she did start. Finally she came out with it so directly she took herself as well as her gran by surprise. "I'm pregnant that's all." She frowned, sighed, still not engaging directly with her grandmother's eyes.

For what seemed like a very long time neither of them spoke. Then Grace said gravely "I see but what I don't see is what you expect me to do about it?"

At last Sam turned to look directly at Grace. "Advice gran, I thought you might give me the benefit of your wisdom."

"I suppose you're talking about abortion young lady, is that it?"

"Well it has to be an option doesn't it? The people at college have intimated indirectly that it could be arranged, through doctors of course."

"The modern age, always an answer for everything these days. Not being much help am I sweetheart?" Her lined face now portrayed feelings of great sadness and she sat there shaking her head slowly from side to side. "I suppose you haven't told your mum and dad yet. You wouldn't be here otherwise I suppose," she added wistfully. The door bell rang.

"That must be my lift gran, I must go."

"Is your lift also the daddy in the matter we've been discussing?" The old lady frowned. "Why not invite him in for a cup of tea dear?"

"I think he'd be a bit shy gran."

"Well at least ask Sam, it's only polite." She frowned in her turn. "Well if you insist but he'll probably want to get away."

Surprisingly the young man at the door did accept the offer of tea. Immediately he appeared inside the room there appeared to be a rapport between him and Sam's grandmother. The three of them chatted casually about life at university in an easy atmosphere with absolutely no mention of pregnancies of course. When they finally left to make the trip back to Sheffield and the old lady was kissing Sam goodbye she whispered in her ear. "He's lovely. Don't know what you're worrying about."

For the first part of the journey back after Kit had said how much he liked Grace the pair of them were quiet although their little problem still hung over them like a sword of Damocles.

Chapter 6

It wasn't exactly the Ritz and she missed Jemma, and the other girls in the halls of residence, but the authorities had made it clear that if she wanted to continue her course then would have to find accommodation off campus. Sadly, and to her intense disappointment and indeed annoyance, Christopher Malpas had declined to share her new flat. She hadn't seen much of him since she'd moved in and was beginning to despair about what was left of their relationship. True he kept insisting that he would take responsibility for the child when it arrived yet with no obvious signs of looking forward to being a father. She sighed when she thought about the boy yet at the same time understood only too well that it had been her decision to carry her pregnancy through to full term whereas dear old Kit supported the procedure for removing the problem from their lives altogether. Yes it seemed she was on her own now backed at a distance by Maggie and Trylon who had applauded her decision to have the baby, showing understanding and kindness when she went home for Christmas.

Her new flat if you could call it that, more like a bedsit really but at least it had a bathroom or at least a shower room which was something, was basic to say the least. She had originally thought of trying to find other students she could share accommodation with but then with a baby due to arrive in a few months decided that wasn't a practical option. The rent was paid for with some money from her parents which Sam knew they couldn't really afford, some from grandma Grace, a little from her grant and a contribution from Christopher. She still cycled into college each day to attend lectures, still joined in some of the college's social activities but nevertheless found it lonely living by herself.

She hadn't been there long when Sophie and Jemma knocked at her door with Ben in tow claiming they were there for a house-warming party, bringing a couple of bottles of wine to support that idea. The girls enthused about the flat almost certainly tongue-in-cheek. It was good to see them anyway.

"Kit not moved in with you then Sam?" Sophie was not a great one when it came to tact.

"He has been round a lot but he's not living here if you must know Sophie." Sophie ignored the look that Jemma aimed in her direction and continued opening one of the bottles they'd brought with them. Ben was going through Sam's small collection of CDs to find some suitable music for a house-warming, something they could dance round to if the mood took them. It was a good evening and Sam enjoyed it but then when they'd gone back came that feeling of loneliness.

And with that came a wave of emotions about Christopher. He hadn't actually ducked his responsibilities in any way yet she was desperately hurt by his attitude towards the impending baby. She could see that a child was not part of his plan for college life, but hell he had appeared to care for her to some degree until he learned of her decision not to have an abortion. Since then their relationship had been awkward to say the least. He still kissed her and had even stayed the night on one occasion but it was all a matter if duty it seemed to Sam and that was very definitely not what she'd expected.

She went to bed that night her thoughts very much governed by her emotions. What was it she'd had with Christopher? Was it love, and if it was, who was loving who. She tried to analyse her own feelings for the father of the child she was carrying and whether they differed between before and after her pregnancy. She was pretty sure they didn't yet now because of her very deep concern about what Kit felt she was beginning to wonder whether she too had changed. She slept alright but woke feeling as if she hadn't, troubled by dreams which she couldn't remember but at the same time unsettled her.

She shivered when she got out of bed and put on her dressing gown. The fierce cold of January was upon them and the only heating in the flat was a single barred electric fire. Kit had promised he would bring her something better from his mother's house, but she was yet to see it. It was another day in college, another day we she might be sitting next to the man who was probably her erstwhile lover. Every time they met now there was an awkwardness between them that didn't auger well for their ongoing association. Ridiculous she knew but she still hankered for a return to what they'd once had.

Anyway no time to reflect on that now she had to get ready for the cycle ride to college in the sneaky wind she could hear blowing against the window. As she showered she ran her hand over her stomach as she did every day trying to detect the first signs of swelling there which would demonstrate to the world that she was pregnant but there was nothing she could feel that cold winter morning. As it happened there was no Christopher in the lecture hall that morning which depressed her somewhat. She had lunch with Jemma but then decided to go back to the flat ostensibly to do some studying instead she ended up watching some mindless thriller on TV.

She might even have dozed off when she was roused from reverie or sleep by a knock on her door. She scrambled to gather herself together before opening the door to find a young man of college age standing there on the threshold grinning like a Cheshire cat.

"Sorry to bother you but is that your bicycle in the hallway?"

Still a trifle dazed Sam took a moment to absorb the question. "Bicycle, bicycle, yes I've got a bike, what of it?"

The boy looked slightly taken aback. Perhaps Sam's tone had been less than sweet. "Yes that one leaning against the wall in the hall. It is rather in the way. Just wondered if you could leave it somewhere else, that's all."

Sam was mildly annoyed now. "And where do you suggest?" She pulled the door wide open. "Not exactly Wembley Stadium in here you know."

The boy's gaze did flit across the interior of Sam's room for just long enough to recognise the presence of a bicycle would hardly be practical. "Yes well sorry to have bothered you, didn't realise, oh forget it, I'm sorry, let's leave it there." He shrugged his shoulders and made to turn away. "Just in case you're interested I'm your neighbour, Jason Anderson at your service. Perhaps we can have a coffee some time, get to know one another." He grinned at her as he started to move across the hallway heading for his own room/.

"What – yes that would be nice. Good night Jason Anderson." She didn't offer her own name despite accepting the fact that she wouldn't mind having coffee with her rather attractive new found neighbour. Tonight though she was tired and anything like a chat over coffee was not a priority.

That wasn't her lasting meeting with the new found neighbour. That came very quickly after the first one. Indeed the very next evening. There he was again, still with the same grin on his face standing at her door. "Look I reckon we got off on the wrong foot last night so I thought, well I thought, neighbours shouldn't be at loggerheads should they? So I went out and bought us a takeaway if you'll do me the honour of dining with me tonight. Only a curry but I've had them from that place before and they're not bad. What do you think – please."

Sam smiled despite herself. It was difficult not to be attracted by this artless young man and what was the harm in sharing a curry with a neighbour. "OK you're on but not for long. I've got an essay to finish tonight. Let me just find my shoes and I'll be with you."

Jason Anderson's room was bigger than hers, a bit untidy but at first glance full of lots of interesting objects, posters and pictures covered the walls, rows of books filled shelves along one side of the room. Above all it was bright and cheerful with three different table lamps giving the place a really cosy atmosphere. Her host appeared full of life, never stopped smiling it seemed. He sat her down at a rather wonky table in the middle of the room and poured her a glass of red wine without asking. Then he was off to his tiny kitchen to retrieve the take-away from the oven. It was but a moment before he was back again.

"Think you'll like this," he said plonking down a plate in front of her. "You at Uni then? What are you studying? You got a boyfriend then? I suppose not or you wouldn't be living alone, gorgeous creature like you." He stopped talking for a short time as he shovelled great mounds of curry into his mouth.

He was right. The curry was good and despite herself Sam found sharing a meal with this ebullient youngster enjoyable.

"Actually I have got a boyfriend but he's based in halls at college and..."

"Strange arrangement that."

"Well maybe it is but then it's a strange situation." Then for reasons she wouldn't be able to fathom later, she blurted out. "I'm pregnant you see and the powers that be thought it better that I look for accommodation off campus."

Jason stopped eating, his eyes searching out hers looking for something in them it seemed. Why on earth had she told this complete stranger about her very private circumstances she couldn't have said. He was a sympathetic seeming chap but surely that wasn't enough reason for her to confide in him.

"Let's forget I told you that Jason, and just enjoy this delicious curry shall we?"

Jason would have liked to ask questions about boyfriends and prospective fathers and so on, but rightly deemed now was not the time.

"All about me so far Jason. What about you? What do you do for a living?"

"Me, bit of a lost soul me. I work in the big bookshop in town for my sins. Never really been sure what I want to do you know. I did go to your place, college I mean, not that long ago, 2.1 in English Literature, thought about writing for a while, still doing a bit, but truth be known I'm rather floating through life at present." Just for a moment his beaming smile vanished and Sam thought he looked just as he'd described himself, a lost soul. She felt a strange feeling inside her that impelled her towards sympathy for this bright young man who appeared to have lost his way in life. She admitted that she found her new-found friend quite beautiful in a male way, a sort of innocent you might say.

"Girlfriend?"

Jason shrugged. "Not really. Some friends who are girls but no one you could really call a girlfriend."

Once again the thought came into Sam's mind that this young man was looking for something although heaven knows what and anyway she certainly wasn't the one to help him find it. "Jason, that was super. I really enjoyed the curry and the wine of course, but I must get back to my essay while I can still think straight."

Jason politely held the door for her as she started her long journey across the hallway back to her own room. He stayed there watching until she closed the door behind her.

Once inside her own room Sam thought back with some amusement to her dinner engagement. She had to admit that she found the young man living across the hall charming. There was no doubt in her mind that she liked him a lot but that was all. There was no way she was going to get entangled with any man as things stood. She may be disappointed with Christopher but like it or not he was the father of this child she was carrying, miserable sod that he had appeared lately. Anyway it was nice to have a new friend. She tackled her essay in a happy frame of mind and went to bed with the pleasant glow of friendship dominating her last wakeful moments.

Things always seem to happen like that. The very night she had invited Jason over to return his dinner invitation Kit had to turn up uninvited. Sam had just served up her chicken casserole cooked in the microwave grandma Grace had given her for Christmas when there was a knock on her door. There he was not looking too happy anyway, raising eyebrows when he saw she had company and only reluctantly accepting her invitation to come in and have a glass of wine. When she introduced the two young men there was no shaking of hands, no smiles, just a slight nod of recognition from both of them.

Sam considered it reasonable to explain the presence of Jason in her room although why she should feel that way she had no idea. After all her erstwhile boyfriend had no rights on her after his decision not to live with her, virtually ending what she at least had thought was a relationship.

"Jason is my neighbour, lives just across the hall."

"Is that right?" Christopher Malpas, her once and she had thought forever, boyfriend, wasn't smiling this evening. He sipped his wine as though it might be poison, his body tense as piano wire. It seemed to Sam that the two men were metaphorically head-butting and just for a fleeting moment she found that funny.

"You going to classes tomorrow Kit?" Sam asked. Anything to ease the tense atmosphere in that small room.

"Of course, why wouldn't I?"

While all this had been going on Jason and Sam had slowly resumed their meal which at least gave then something to do while Christopher with only a glass of wine watched and waited although exactly what he was waiting for was unclear. The fact was he had come round to speak to Sam about something important, and was waiting for his moment. Jason wondered if their visitor was hanging on because his presence blocked what might be considered his rival from having a clear field? Either way Jason concluded that was or had been something more than casual friendship between the two. Being of tactful disposition he eventually got to his feet, mumbled something about having to get back and left Sam with an angry Kit to sort out whatever problems they had between them.

"That was a great stew Sam. Keep me going for a week that will, thanks a million." He appeared glad to get away. The door had no sooner closed behind the departing Jason before Sam turned an angry face towards to her other visitor. "That wasn't great Chistopher. You chased the poor boy away and after all he was my guest – not on was it?"

"Don't know what he was doing here anyway."

That was it. Sam was by nature an even tempered girl but that comment really got up her nose. Moreover it had the added affect of bringing others matters between them to a head. "Just you listen to me Kit. You've made it quite clear that our relationship, as it was, no longer exists and yet you come charging in here objecting to my having a meal and a glass of wine with another bloke. Talk about dog in the manger." Her face went red with the sheer passion of her indignation.

"You're going to have my child."

"That is a fact, but what a bloody reluctant father to be you are. How can you claim to have any rights when you virtually deserted that child's mother?"

Chapter 7

Since moving in with Jason Sam had felt a lot happier, less lonely and more settled in her life. Being the honest girl she was Sam had already spilled the beans about her pregnancy so there were no secrets to be revealed before accepting Jason's invitation to live with him. He had shrugged the revelation away with his usual easy-going manner saying babies took a long time to hatch and there was plenty of time to make decisions in the months to come. She was slightly worried about what Maggie and Trylon would say, or at least think, when she told them of her new arrangement. After all two live-in boyfriends in the short time since she'd been at Uni may not look quite right to them.

As might have been expected Christopher Malpas was furious about her decision, at first storming at both Sam and her new boyfriend, if that's what he was, followed by a period of silence. Since that initial series of outbursts they hadn't heard anything from him at all which caused Sam some concern. He was the father of the baby she was carrying, he did have rights which would be become more relevant once the baby was born. Any discussion about that critical time had been brushed aside by Jason saying they should live for the moment and enjoy loving each other while they both felt that way inclined.

Sam still saw Kit at lectures and although he largely steered clear of her he did sometimes ask how she was. There was no warmth in his enquiries. How could two people change so much in a short space of time from almost frantic lovers to almost strangers was a troubling thought for Sam. Anyway she had Jason now and although they hadn't declared any undying love for each other they were pals as well as lovers and that, for now, made for a pleasant existence. Of course what would happen when a baby arrived on the scene was a matter yet to be considered.

They were in the park. Spring sunshine pleasantly warming their walk when Sam stopped and turned to face Jason with a serious look on her face that foretold some serious words to come.

"You know Jason, sweet boy that you are, we haven't really discussed the matter of this child growing inside me."

"What is there to discuss? You're going to have a baby. So what – it's happened before all over the world you know and the earth has never stopped turning yet. There was that infectious grin again."

"Very true although in this case you're not the father yet you appear to be prepared to accept part of the responsibility that will be involved in having a child around."

"We should get a larger flat, two bedrooms, don't you think?"

"I'm not talking about accommodation Jason, more about the rights and wrongs of the case. That sod Christopher Malpas should be supporting me, but there you have it; he isn't. But why should you? We've only known each other a few months and having a baby wherever the location is a big thing."

"Don't you love me Sam?" The look in the boy's eyes could only be described as soulful.

In fact it was a very good question. Sam liked him a lot but was she in love with him? That was something she'd been asking herself for weeks. The guy had come along and offered her a kind of sanctuary when she was feeling lonely and deserted and for that she would be eternally grateful but still the question did you love him? It was a big ask to saddle a man about whom she couldn't answer that rather basic question, with all that was associated with the birth of a baby and all that transpired from that. Jason appeared to be unfazed by the idea of having a new born in the flat even if that was one they'd chosen together. And then there was Christopher, an unresolved factor in the affair. He's always said he would stand by his responsibilities but how on earth was it all going to fit together?

Sam went home at Easter taking Jason with her. They travelled in his old unreliable MG, his pride and joy. On this occasion the journey went off without a hitch. Maggie and Trylon were delighted to see Sam and cautiously pleased to see Jason as well although maybe a trifle unsure of his status. They were in the kitchen about to have a cup of tea, Jason had disappeared into the bathroom.

"Don't think I'm interfering sweetie but is that young man the daddy?"

What a question that was. If only Maggie knew.

"It's complicated mum. The answer to your question is 'no' but having said that Jason and I are partners."

"I see." But of course she didn't see at all and the expression on her face showed her bewilderment.

"I'll tell you all about us later mum. For the time being let's just have that cup of tea you promised shall we?"

Sam did explain to her parents later that evening that she was living with Jason, that they were good friends, that he knew about the baby, and was quite prepared to be something like a surrogate father to the child when it arrived. When it came to Christopher Malpas she found it more difficult to explain his attitude. "You see he didn't want me to have the baby although to be fair he accepts his share of the responsibility. What's less certain is how he will react once he's actually a dad. We have talked of course but so far he's not come up with how he feels about it."

On the drive back Jason was in high spirits. "I enjoyed meeting your parents Sam. Your mum reminds me of mine."

Surprisingly that was the first time he had ever mentioned his own family and equally surprisingly she had never asked until now. "Where do your parents live Jason?"

The boy's eyes turned away from the road to look her in the eye. "No idea where my dad is, my mum died three years ago, cancer I'm afraid."

Eyes back on the road but before that she had seen the pain in them. No wonder he'd never discussed his family before.

After that short dramatic interlude they drove on, each with their own thoughts until the relaxing tone of the engine noise changed as they neared Tamworth. There was an unhealthy sound to the engine now as the power fell away and they drifted to a halt. "Sorry Sam, appears the old girl isn't' feeling too well." Said with a grimace of apology.

Jason quickly had the bonnet up rummaging around in the engine trying to detect the fault. It wasn't long before he was back in the driver's seat, his face a picture of regretful apology. "Sorry love no road side rescue, didn't think it was worth it but there you are."

They did find a local taxi on the net which was why they were sitting in the old world bar drinking pints of beer in the Green Man in the middle of nowhere. The landlord had already told Jason that there was a garage only two or three miles away but when he rang them they refused to do anything that evening although they agreed somewhat grudgingly to come out the next day and take a look at Jason's sick motor.

It hadn't taken long for Jason's sunny disposition to come to the surface. "You've got yourself a right fool here Samantha. That old bus of mine was just waiting to kick the bucket and I refused to accept that the poor old thing wouldn't last forever." He appeared to accept the inevitable without much resentment at the fates.

"Perhaps it can be repaired Jason. Why do you assume the worst?"

"Because dear girl if I do that and things turn out better than expected it's a pleasant surprise rather than a disappointment; quite logical really." His grin was infectious. She felt affection for this unworldly young man welling up inside her. Perhaps she was in love with the guy despite a feeling of anxiety about what would happen to the two of them once a baby arrived on the scene and of course there was also Christopher Malpas bound to be part of that equation.

The next day it was as Jason had feared, his old friend was a write off. He sold it for scrap and they caught a train from Tamworth back home to Sheffield.

Chapter 8

Sam spent some time during her summer break from Sheffield University at home with Maggie and Trylon during which time the signs of her baby began to show. Maggie spent some time trying to persuade her daughter that when the time came for the birth she should return home to have the child rather than in some hospital far away up North. Sam said she would have to get used to being a single mother and that must start where she intended to live which of course was Sheffield. She was not going to let the little matter of a child interfere with her plans to get a First.

"Is that Jason chap going to stick by you darling when there's a howling baby on the scene?"

"He says he will, mum, and he's already looking for a larger flat, one with two bedrooms." That's what she said but it didn't stop her wondering how long that placid young man would put up with such a dramatic change in their lives. After all he really had no responsibility in the affair did he?

She remembered that conversation she'd had with her mother at the beginning of the autumn term. Now, this morning, dragging her considerable belly with her wherever she went, she bumped into Kit Malpas. She thought it was just 'bumped into' but later she thought perhaps it was more contrived than that.

There was a frown on Christopher's face. "You're looking very well Sam."

"Yes I've been lucky as far as health all through my pregnancy."

The boy was uneasy about something. "Look Sam can we have a talk sometime, a proper talk, just the two of us?"

They were outside the lecture hall when the meeting, contrived or otherwise, took place. Naturally Sam agreed to have a chat at lunch time with the father of her very impending child, little imagining that what he had to say would cause her so much turmoil.

After the lecture had ended Sam and Kit met up in the Arts Tower Cafe as agreed. Settled with bagels and coffee in front of them she waited to learn what was important enough for Kit to want to meet up after all his many absences in the last eight and a bit months.

"Look Sam I was wrong, wrong all along the line. I treated you abominably and I want to do something about it now."

Sam kept quiet, sure there was more to follow that strained little speech. "Yes, well, now I've seen the light I'm ready to shack up with you. I've been looking around at flats in the city and come up with a few for you to look at if you'll agree."

To say Sam was shocked would be to put it very mildly indeed. The bloody nerve of the man; after months of aggressive behaviour and total lack of consideration for her feelings here he was trying very belatedly to take control. She was very angry of course, but then there was always that very important factor to consider which was that he, whatever might or might not be agreed between them, was the impending child's father. "You must be fucking kidding Christopher. It's a bit late in the day to come up with this now."

He looked sheepish as she lashed at him with her tongue. "You're right of course. I'm just a bloody fool but when it happened it seemed to ruin all my best laid plans as Burns might have said and then my mum......."

"Oh I see, this change of heart is down to your mum is it? Your mum telling you what a bastard you are. Really Kit you can do better than that can't you?"

"My change of heart is nothing to do with my mother I can assure you Sam. I was only going to say that she's offered to help with the rent for a flat for us."

Sam supposed it was understandable that Christopher should have told his mother about the child, but nevertheless there was still a factor of control in there somewhere which she didn't much like. Anyway all that didn't matter she was with gentle Jason now and that was that.

"All too late Christopher. Jason and I are quite happy as we are and he's quite ready to be a surrogate dad. And as far as flats are concerned we think we've already found a suitable two bed place within easy reach of the college."

That wasn't entirely true. The fact was that they were looking at a list of potential places but had yet to make a decision.

Kit shrugged. "Look Samantha I'm trying to do the right thing by you and the baby. Surely you agree that a child's father should be living together with it's mother."

Sam sighed. She understood that in some ways the bloke was right but it was all too late now wasn't it? "You should have thought about this eight months ago. It's all too late now."

"Why? I'm sure you could put the case to that Jason guy that it's better for the baby that she or he lives with its dad."

"Forget it Christopher, I'm not changing my mind at this late stage." That's what she said but deep inside her brain thoughts were tumbling round like clothes in a washing machine. She had found Kit very attractive until his violent reaction to her pregnancy had changed everything round. Jason was a sweet, faithful boy but was her relationship of the same degree of passion as with her first love? Quite a dilemma and one she didn't relish.

Back in the flat that evening Sam was subdued to say the least. "What gives sweetie, you look down in the dumps?"

Sam was hurting. She knew that to go back to Christopher Malpas would break Jason's heart yet the temptation to shack up with the father of her baby was hugely attractive. The child would need his real dad not a surrogate however well-meaning.

"I'm fine love, hectic day at college, got an essay to finish before tomorrow that's all."

Jason looked sceptical but left it at that at least for the time being. Later that night when they were in bed together she couldn't rid herself over the doubts of which way to turn about her future and that of her baby. She lay awake long after she believed Jason was asleep and then in the early hours she felt his arms creep round her and his quiet voice asking again what was wrong. This time she told him all about her meeting with Kit Malpas. His body went rigid. "And I suppose you're thinking it would be best for the baby to be living with his real dad."

When she reached out to touch his face Sam could feel the wetness on his cheeks and knew that what she was going to do was just about the cruelest thing she'd ever done in her life. Despite that bitter thought she knew then that her decision was made.

Morning came. Sam understood that her night–time decision now had to be turned into concrete action. Jason didn't have to be told, he knew what was going to happen and it turned that easy-going young man into a picture of abject misery. "I had thought....." he started to say. Then shook his head in seeming bewilderment.

"I know Jason, I really do know. I'm a total cow and I deserve anything you choose to throw at me."

"What's the point of that. You've made your decision and that's that – lucky bastard - that Christopher Malpas."

That was all that was said that bleak morning. As she cycled to college she felt the first hint of Autumn chill in the air. Now she would have to impart her decision on to that sod Christopher Malpas. He didn't deserve her, but there you are, deserve or not she had now committed herself to moving in with her baby's dad and who knows what might follow. There was going to be awkwardness at first that was for sure, but she had once loved the boy or thought she had. What did she feel now? That was a very big question, a question that was causing her deep trepidation. Should she have made that momentous decision without being absolutely sure of her feelings towards Christopher Malpas.

Sam buttonholed Kit at the start of the lecture they were both attending. A serious bit of talking was required so they agreed that they would drive out to some country pub in the old Riley to have that serious talk. Christopher was in high spirits understanding quite rightly that this talking thing Sam had proposed meant she was up for his cohabiting suggestion. He felt a trifle guilty because truth was his change of mind with regard to his approach to

Sam had been largely brought about by a series of quiet, very serious, conversations with his mother. He still had doubts in his own mind yet his course of action would go ahead despite those doubts. Where it would all lead was quite another matter.

Once ensconced in the snug bar of the Crescent Moon with beer for Christopher and lime and lemonade for Sam in front of them there was something of a hiatus.

Then Kit began with a repeat of his previous apology about how he'd been an ignorant bastard with regard to his attitude towards Sam's pregnancy and his reasons for that attitude.

"I'm so sorry to have messed up your plans for college life." Sam thought a touch of sarcasm was justified in the circumstances. "And how is it different now Kit?"

"Perhaps I've grown up a bit."

"Or your mum has told you to do the right thing."

That barb had struck home yet there was no way he was going to admit that his change of heart had anything at all to do with his mother. He spread some brochures on the table in front of them like a magician producing a rabbit out of a hat. "Have a look at these, see what you think."

Sam brushed them aside. "Let's face it Christopher I haven't decided yet whether living with you would work after your previous performance. I think we should talk about that before we consider places to live, don't you?"

"We did get on pretty well before Sam, didn't we?"

"Different circumstances then." Her normally pretty face didn't look so pretty right at that moment as she scowled across the table at the young man who was offering to do the right thing but of whom she still had serious doubts. Would he get up and run at the first sign of difficulty were they to live together. She had trusted lovely Jason over the last few months and now here she was considering dumping him in favour of the bloke who had done the dumping when she got pregnant with his child.

"I can't keep on saying I'm sorry Sam. Please let's try and make a go of it. I'm really very fond of you."

Sam sighed, shook her head."You could have fooled me." She was bitter but then what was the point of harking back. She believed every child should have two parents on the spot as it were to bring him or her up, and support them through childhood. Perhaps that would work if Christopher really had made up his own mind and not been coerced into action by his mother. She picked up one of the brochures from the table in front of her. "I suppose we could take a look at a couple of them, no promises, just look." Simple statement yet it represented a decision in all probability.

In fact that was what happened. They found a flat not far from college. When Christopher drove her round to the place she shared with Jason to collect her things the boy was all smiles, friendly and helpful, yet Sam was sure you saw tears behind the smiles. She knew he was hurting. She was hurting herself, but this was something she had to get through now she had made the decision to live with Kit. Back in the new flat the atmosphere was tense. It was months ago that they had been lovers and now here they were in the position of lovers with neither showing any signs of wanting to renew their earlier passion.

They went shopping like a together couple each anxious to pander to the other's desires as far as food and drink went. The atmosphere here lightened a touch when Kit bought some flowers which he insisted were for Sam. "Brighten the place up a bit," was all he said yet in fact the action spoke much louder than words.

Back at the flat Sam volunteered to cook their first meal together. "Only if you're prepared to put your life in my hands," she joked. How hard could it be to cook sausages and mash. True the sausages were a bit burnt but they were both hungry so what's a bit of burnt skin when you're famished. The bottle of Chianti they bought while out shopping helped a bit. They were still on edge, not sure how to act with each other in this slightly artificial situation. They were ultra considerate, desperately polite but where was the passion and intimacy of partners expecting their first child?

It became even more problematic when bedtime arrived. There was only one bed in the flat and the sofa in the living room was small and unlikely to provide a comfortable night's sleep. Each made their bathroom visits emerging dressed in their pyjamas and quietly sliding under the substantial duvet to lie some way apart. Truth was that Sam's libido had been at a high level particularly high as her pregnancy progressed. Now in bed with a man whose body she had been familiar with in the past she wasn't going to sleep without some sexual intimacy. Once she had made the first move by running her hand up Kit's thigh to his groin it was all passion. The cautious approach of earlier in the day was abandoned in favour of full-blooded sex. And it did more than satisfy their individual sexual needs. It established the basis of a relationship for the days to come. Days in which they would become parents with all that involved.

Later lying awake in the new bed, with Christopher gently snoring at her side, Sam felt a sense of relief coming over her. A sense that things were now as they should be with the father of her child living in as it were. Her feelings for him were almost certainly loving. A feeling that he appeared to reciprocate earlier that evening. Yet she wasn't stupid. She understood that living together

Roy Grantham

as a couple would involve some adjustments on both sides and more so once they had three persons in the household.

Chapter 9

Of course she knew, had always known, giving birth was a painful operation, but hell this was worse than she'd expected and why did it take so fucking long. She was certain the baby wanted out and she definitely wanted the damn thing out, so why all this painful delay. It was now in the delivery room that she hoped the hours of waiting would soon be over. The midwife kept peering at her vulva and muttering about degrees of dilation all the while keeping up a cheerful banter.

"Not long to go now sweet child."

She was Jamaican, full of smiles and caring assurances which is more than could be said for Christopher who hovered by the bed apparently reluctantly holding her hand, grimacing when she clenched hard as yet another spasm overtook her.

"I just love to see them babies arrive, just like pearls out of an oyster, and just as precious."

Fuck the seafood analogy thought Sam, let's get this damn thing on the road. She's been told that the epidural would significantly reduce the pain level. My God she thought it must hurt a bit without it then. Then it came to the point where the midwife was telling her to push. No results the first couple of times and then delighted cries of here he comes. Sam couldn't see what was going on between her legs but she could see Kit's face which was screwed up in something like horror as he glanced down every so often at what was happening before his reluctant eyes. Then came the victory shout from the midwife. "A beautiful baby boy, you lucky lady, all over now and you have a son." Sam knew she had something because there it was yelling like a banshee. She slumped back and closed her eyes, felt Kit's lips on her own and was glad.

"You coming with me to watch me check over this young man?" Kit realised the midwife was talking to him and followed her bulky backside out of the delivery room down the corridor to another room where his son was gently bathed and checked to make sure everything was where it should be. As he lay naked on the table now all clean and shining his little penis suddenly produced a spurt of urine which arched gracefully through the air. "Well at least there's nothing wrong with that part of the child." The midwife seemed to find the whole experience of delivering a baby into the hands of its worried parents to be one of delighted joy.

"You want to hold the little man daddy?"

Christopher Malpas, father of one, gingerly took the baby in his arms under the careful instruction about how to hold him from the beaming midwife. He was then instructed to take the infant back to Sam who in the meantime had slept a little but was now ready to take her son into her arms, her face a picture of amazement at what she had achieved.

"You can try to feed him if you like, see if he's interested."

After a few attempts the baby got the idea and began to suck enthusiastically at the nipple of Sam's right breast, a sight that brought mixed thoughts into Kit's already tangled mind. It struck him then that he should be kissing the mother of this greedy little bundle of humanity. Sam accepted the kiss, her eyebrows raised quizzically, her smile nevertheless hopeful.

Shortly after they moved Sam into the main ward and told her she could go home tomorrow. 'Home' Sam thought. A strange flat, a stitched together relationship, no family around her. Then to her delight Maggie and Trylon were there as if by magic at the side of her bedside. That was one good mark for Kit she supposed. Her parents were staying at a hotel in the city centre having arrived the previous day and been kept informed by Kit of the actual time of the birth of their gorgeous little grandson.

They all met up the next day after Christopher had picked up his new family from the hospital. Maggie did a personal tour of the flat that was now the youngsters' home.

"And where my I ask is this one going to sleep?" Maggie was cradling the little boy in her arms in a way that suggested she never wanted to let him go. "And what's more what are you going to call the little chap?"

The new parents had very belatedly discussed names but had made no decision as yet. When Sam suggested Jason a look of horror spread over Kit's face until he had realised she was joking.

"Not very original I suppose but I like James."

A rather hectic discussion followed with everyone putting forward their own ideas. It was brought to a halt when the door bell rang. There on the doorstep stood Edith Malpas looking a trifle hesitant. "Just had to come and see my new grandson."

After introductions any initial awkwardness soon vanished beneath the torchlight of mutual admiration for the new baby. Maggie brought up the question of sleeping arrangements for the new arrival again and when Sam said they intended to let the baby sleep in his carry-cot for the time being, she dragged Trylon out to visit the shops to purchase a cot right there and then. Edith not to be outdone went off with them eager to add her contribution to the child's welfare. That left Sam and Christopher alone with their son. There were indulgent smiles when the boy started crying and satisfaction once he was given a breast to suck. As Sam sat there feeding her baby in an almost dreamlike state her thoughts were confused. Yes of course she loved this little mite sucking at her teat, yet her life was now changed to such a degree she had never thought possible. She glanced across at Christopher who was watching her from the other armchair and wondered what he thought about their new joint circumstances. She worried that he might have been coerced by his mother into doing the right thing. Was he really committed to being a father? He smiled back at her, a smile that gave her hope.

When the assorted parents returned with their gifts for the newborn there was renewed excitement for a while as the cot emerged from its packaging. Sam unwrapped the delightful mobile, other baby toys and a baby monitor. By then it was dinner time and the two older women set about preparing the evening meal in an atmosphere of excited happiness. It's amazing how a new baby can bring all that about by just lying there and gazing into thin air.

Sam enjoyed being the second most important object of attention, enjoyed the wine. More than that she loved having her parents there so obviously delighted with their grandchild and pleased also that Edith was also obviously thrilled by the birth although she did with reluctance late in the evening say she had to make a start on her way back to Scunthorpe. Shortly after her departure Trylon and Maggie made their way back to their hotel. After all the excitement and genuine joy it was a comedown to be in that small flat, just the two of them and a sleeping baby. On a whim Sam decided she needed some fresh air and got up from her chair to grab a coat needed to protect her from the cold night air. Kit yawned. "Be my guest."

As she walked down the street Samantha noticed for the first time the name sign on the side of a building. Norton Road it said. She'd been living here for weeks and this was the first time she had known the name of the street in which she was dwelling. She had a little chuckle to herself. It struck her then that the last few weeks now seemed like a dream. She, a university student, twenty years old was now a mother. She couldn't believe it and halted her walk under a lamppost to think harder to make sure she wasn't still in that dream. She shivered in the yellow light wondering just what the fates had in store for her. Then her thoughts drifted back to earlier in the day when Edith came out with a quiet question which stopped them all in their tracks. "You two going to tie the knot then?" Conversation in the room came to an abrupt halt. "Sorry out of order, should mind my own business I guess." No one said anything in response to Edith's comment but when Sam looked across at her partner all she saw was a deep frown which made her wonder not for the first time just how committed was Christopher Malpas to his new role as a father and how far his decision has been influenced by his mother's coercion.

She was tired, the cold was getting through to her bones. She turned back down Norton Road towards her new home and her new baby All those thought put right to the back of her mind for now at least. The baby was still asleep when she got home and so was Kit. She took the opportunity to slip into their minute bathroom. She was worried about her tummy, it still seemed to her to be too

83

fat even without a baby inside it. She looked in the small mirror on the wall to take a closer look but couldn't see properly so she took off her clothes, climbed on the small stool to stand sideways to get a good profile of her stomach. She sniffed. Yes it was extended but then perhaps that was normal after a birth. Had her mum been there she would have asked her the question.

Yesterday had all been about family. Today it was friends wanting a glimpse of the newborn. Jemma, Sophie and Ben all arrived together bearing flowers and small gifts. Earlier on that morning Maggie and Trylon had popped in to say goodbye before starting their long journey back home, but now it was all about youth and a degree of wonder that one of their kind had jumped the gun as it were producing a child after only one year at college. The visitors were still passing the baby from one set of arms to another when another caller rang the bell.

"You old bugger. You a dad, strike me dead." Lionel clapped his brother on the back and handed over a bottle of champagne, his face lit up by a smile of delight or maybe it was astonishment.

The small flat was filled with the sound of voices enjoying the atmosphere of celebration, music was playing, the baby was lying in the carrycot staring up as though bewildered by this new world into which he had been ejected and which was still a complete mystery to him. Then above the happy chatter the doorbell rang again.

There on the doorstep stood Jason, bunch of flowers in one hand, large paper bag in the other. The young man looked lost when Sam invited him in. The noise of a moment ago had subsided and everyone stood there not quite sure how to react. They all knew of Sam's previous association with the newcomer so it shouldn't have been all that surprising that he wanted to see his ex-girlfriend's baby. Yet there was tension, perhaps even danger lurking in the air. Christopher didn't look pleased to see Jason as he made a clumsy effort to hug Sam and kiss her on the cheek, dropping the parcel in the process.

"And this is James," Sam offered the child to Jason like a sacrificial lamb.

Were those tears in his eyes, maybe. Whatever his outward appearance Sam knew full well that her ex-flatmate was deeply moved at the sight of the baby.

It turned out that the large bag contained a soft toy rabbit, far too big for a baby but the kindness of the action very nearly had Sam in tears. The decision to move in with Kit had been desperately difficult. She still had strong feelings for gentle Jason which was how she always thought of him. The late arrival stood there awkwardly with a glass of champagne in his hand as the conversation around the room took hold again. A tense looking Kit was still frowning, not joining in the general chat, giving the impression that he was waiting for Jason to go.

Chapter 10

"Something amusing you Dr. Jollison?"

Sam's tutor was indeed smiling. "No not really. I'm just amazed that's all. I'm told you became a mum only two weeks ago and here you are armed with essays and looking great. How the hell do you do it Samantha?"

She returned the smile. She liked the man and often enjoyed a bit of age difference banter with him. "Well I'm lucky I suppose. James, that's the baby, sleeps a lot and he's being looked after part time in a very good nursery only two street away from my flat so I manage to combine motherhood and study OK, so far at least."

That's what she said although she couldn't help her thoughts flitting back over the last few days. Learning about babies, putting up with Christopher's complaints about the baby crying and the smell when he had to be changed. She sometimes thought that her partner in this parenting thing saw it as a great burden he had to carry because of a commitment to some sort of the right thing to do rather than to the excitement of being part of a new family. Well she was in it now whatever the 'it' was.

Sam had arranged to meet Kit in the car park so they could both travel back to the flat together but when she got there at the allotted time there was no sign of the Riley. It was cold, it began to rain, Sam was peeved off to say the least. She hung round for another twenty minutes before giving up and running for the bus by which time she was soaked and she still had to pick up James from the nursery.

Half an hour later, dried out and with a sleeping baby in his cot, Sam had calmed down to some extent so that when she heard the key in the door her initial fury had also lessened to a degree.

"Sam I'm so sorry. I got hooked up with an argument with the lads and completely lost track of the time."

"Lost track of your mobile too I suppose?"

Christopher really did look contrite, yet Sam sensed there was a hint of annoyance at what he perceived as her anger although she hadn't yet said a word.

"You fucking selfish bugger. You knew I was waiting, you probably knew it was raining. No one loses that much sense of the time. Just go to hell."

She couldn't help but think wistfully of the time she had spent with Jason and his gentle consideration with regard to everything about their relationship. Yet what was the point, the die was cast, the baby wanted feeding, someone had to prepare a meal.

The next thing was the car. Christopher's beloved Riley. Sam wanted to go home for Christmas and although that was some time ahead the question of how to get down to Devon had already raised its head.

"What about my mum? She'll be upset if she doesn't see James over the holiday."

"Yes Kit I understand that and we will go round to see her during the holiday, but I promised Maggie I would be there for Christmas Day. Anyway that still leaves usith the problem of transport doesn't it?"

Roy Grantham

Christopher looked at her with a look of horror in his eyes. "For God's sake Sam you're not asking me to get rid of my motor are you?"

Sam pursed her lips, gave a little shrug of the shoulders. "Well I know you love that old car but it's not really suitable for babies is it? You do have a baby you know, not that you appear to want to get very involved."

"What do you mean? I changed his nappy last night didn't I?"

A little half-laugh from Sam. "Yes I can't deny it but how often have you done so. You're supposed to share the work not just make a gesture now and then."

Kit sulked for the rest of the evening but unbeknown to Sam he had already come to a very reluctant conclusion that his beautiful Riley would have to go. They would need other transport and anyway the old lady was beginning to cost a fortune in repairs. In his own mind he still felt that he had been coerced into this current relationship. The truth was that his earlier passion for Sam had not been completely resurrected by the fact of them sharing a flat and a child. It was worrying to say the least, obligation versus wish for freedom. Freedom he didn't know he had until he found now he was bound by the chains of responsibility. It didn't auger well for the future happiness of this particular young couple yet neither considered coming out and saying so.

Three days before Christmas all three of the little family were driving down to Devon in a Toyota Yaris Hatchback with lots of miles on the clock but in good condition according to Christopher's brother who claimed to know something about cars. The £1655 it cost was paid for with a loan from Mrs. Malpas which was one very good reason why they would need to travel back north before the holiday was over to let the good woman see her only grandson.

Naturally Maggie and Trylon were delighted to have them to stay for Christmas, putting up with the baby crying and Christopher sulking without a qualm.

"How are the two of you getting on with your studies now you have the distraction of this young man on the scene?" A fairly neutral question you might think yet it brought a frown to Kit's handsome face.

It wasn't him however that answered the question. "We're getting into a new way of working and living," responded Sam brightly, suggesting that babies weren't really a bar to learning. The truth was that they were, particularly when the partner in question didn't contribute his fair share of time to looking after their child.

The holiday did pass off quite well despite Kit's continued mourning for his Riley. It's amazing how alcohol will lift the mood. Maggie tired herself out making sure that everyone had a good time while Trylon tried to build up a rapport with Christopher even to the extent of taking him out to the pub one evening for a couple of pints of beer. The boy himself emerged from his disconsolate state of mind from time to time during which times Sam recognised what she'd seen in him in the first place. And his pride in his little son was real enough even though quietly expressed.

After Christmas dinner they strolled out in the cold crisp air with baby James wrapped up and cosy in his new buggy, one of the presents coming the way of the young couple from Sam's proud parents. When Maggie slipped her arm through Christopher's he didn't resist. Perhaps his feeling of resentment at being railroaded into accepting his responsibilities of being a father was weakening. Anyway it was difficult not to like Maggie and what's more he rather liked feeling part of such a welcoming family.

"You're a lucky boy you know Christopher. Lucky I mean to be the dad of such a glorious little boy and to have Sam of course, although I admit to being just a little bit biased." She looked up into his face smiling her good will and Kit for all his doubts couldn't resist smiling back. Yes he liked Maggie well enough, but remained uncertain about the strength of his feelings for her daughter.

All in all the holiday went well and Christopher surprised himself in having enjoyed his stay with the amiable Makepeaces. When they set out for their journey back to Sheffield there were tears but then as the Toyota sped out of sight Maggie put her arms round Trylon to give him a hug of what might almost be called satisfaction with the way the holiday had worked out and more important the way the two young people appeared ready to make a go of their relationship. Maggie would have liked to see them married although love was what counted and she reckoned that was there if a trifle strained at times. It would grow stronger with time was her view.

Chapter 11

Tact was the byword. Sam looked across at her partner's face and recognised the hurt. "Well done Kit, you deserved it, worked hard for it."

He sniffed. "Not a first though is it?"

"I doubt whether it makes much difference. I mean between a 2-1 and a first when it comes to jobs and that."

James sensed there was something not quite right in the air and moved in to rest his head against his mother's thigh. "Mummy," he murmured anxiously.

She laughed and rumpled his hair. "It's alright darling, nothing to worry about. Do you want your breakfast now?"

They had both gone to three career days during their final time at college. Subject to him getting at least a 2-1 Christopher had been accepted on a graduate training course for large paper making company which would mean them moving away from their home in Sheffield. Sam rather liked the idea of becoming a social worker but decided to bide her time until after they'd made their move down to Kent. Relations between the two young people were not all they might be but for now they had no plans to alter that relationship such as it was. They made love regularly, they were in the main polite to each other, they accepted things as they were yet somehow the romance was gone.

The D.S. Smith HR department had arranged a flat for them in Sittingbourne free of charge for three months to give them chance to look around and decide where they actually wanted to live. The flat was in a large old building near the centre of the town, very clean and well furnished but obviously lacking any individuality. They hadn't needed a moving van to change homes, cramming all their meagre possessions into the Toyota.

Sam stood in the centre of their new living room and looked about her while James ran around the various rooms excited by this change of a home.

"What do you think then?"

"It'll be fine when we unpack a few of our things and spread then around." Sam was determined to give their new location a chance although from what they'd seen of Sittingbourne so far she didn't think much of it.

As if guessing her thoughts Chris said with a faint smile, "We don't have to stay in Sittingbourne you know but let's face it three months rent free is worth having. Isn't it?"

Sam had to get James something to eat so kept her thoughts to herself. "Fine. You unpack while I get some food ready." They had stopped off at Tesco and grabbed a bag full of shopping on the way to the flat only to find that Chris's efficient new company HR department already stocked the fridge and some of the kitchen cupboards with basic food supplies. "Kind of them don't you think?"

"Well they want to make sure their new guy is well looked after. After all I am on what they call a fast track graduate training course and they want to make sure I'm off to a good start." There was humour in there somewhere and the smiles they exchanged relaxed the mild tension that had accompanied their arrival at the new flat.

"Mummy I'm starving hungry."

The next day Christopher went off to make his first appearance in his new job. Usually confident, that morning he frowned his unease, holding Sam close in his arms for some time as he said his goodbyes. Thinking about it afterwards Sam concluded that their partnership did mean something to them both despite the fading away of what might be called their honeymoon period.

She had in mind that today she would check out estate agents and nurseries in Sittingbourne. The former in case they decided to make their home elsewhere and the latter in case they decided to stay in the town, That obliging HR department had left a lot of leaflets and information sheets about the locality waiting for them when they arrived. It was late April but still quite chilly so she wrapped James up warm and loaded him into his buggy despite protests from him that he wanted to walk.

It proved a tiring day traipsing round the different addresses with a child fluctuating between being tired and wanting to walk and generally not finding the whole exercise very entertaining. Eventually Sam had had enough and returned to their temporary home loaded with brochures and other sources of information to allow James to unpack his box of toys and to watch CBBC which kept him quiet while she made herself a cup of tea and started to wade through the mountain of literature.

She hadn't even got round to thinking about her own job search yet. First things first and at least they had some money coming in and a free flat for three months so there was time, yet there was an urge somewhere inside her to get started on her own career. She loved James with all her

heart but there was no way she intended to be a stay-at –
home mum; that was a certainty.

When Christopher came back to the flat after his first
day in the job Sam determined to be kind knowing the
stress he had probably been under. Thoughts of nurseries
and place to live would have to wait.

"How did it go then?"

Her partner shook his head in a dazed fashion as he
slumped back into one of the two armchairs that came
with the flat. James had torn himself away from the box
and now came into the room and jumped into his father's
lap causing him to wince from the impact. "Where you
been Daddy?"

Kit ruffled the youngster's hair. "I've been to work
James. Someone has to earn a crust to keep you in fish
fingers you know."

"What a crust Daddy? What's work?"

Sam felt a surge of affection for the two of them, a
feeling that families were quite wonderful things. "Can I
get you a beer or something Chris?"

The new employee blew his lips out in a weary
gesture. "You know Sam, it's all so bloody strange, a
million things to know. I should have done more
homework about the paper industry before I signed up to
that course. Nice enough bunch though. I suppose I'll just
have to give it time."

Sam came across and sat on the arm of his chair, her
sympathy mode to the fore. Chris slumped against her, his
head resting on her breasts seeking solace in her
femininity. Then as though coming to some sort of
conclusion he raised his head and smiled at her. "Where's
this bloody beer then woman?"

"Coming your honour." She laughed. Both had had weary days but for the time being their rapport was strong and Sam liked that.

The next day when Christopher had gone off to work again Sam's thought turned to her own career. On the career days at college she had gleaned some information about working in the social services. She understood there would be rigorous training and then she would need to register with The General Social Care Council before she could work in the sector. What she didn't know were the specific details applying to the area where she was now living. She made a few calls and was invited to call at the local council offices for a chat. No it didn't matter if she brought her young son with her she was told.

The woman she met came over as very stern, thick-lens spectacles making her eyes look enormous as she indicated a chair. Sam sat, unsure of her welcome, with her little son on her knee, waiting until the dragon finished reading some papers on her desk. Then, when the woman smiled, she looked altogether different. She came out from behind her great desk, held out her hand to be shaken, chucked James under the chin and asked him what his name was. The boy turned his head away, nestling into Sam's chest.

Back behind her fortress, Mrs. Harper flipped though the resume Sam had presented. "A first eh, very impressive, but as I'm sure you know social work has little to do with academia although there will be a lot more of that before you're qualified. However I have some good news for you. There is a very significant shortage of social workers in our area and I can enrol you on a two year course instead of the usual three because of that. Hard work though, virtually degree level although I don't suppose you'll have much trouble with that." She handed over some literature amongst which was an application for the course in question to start in the Autumn at a college in Faversham. "You'll have no problem in being accepted on the course I can assure you but please discuss it with friends and family before making up your mind. I don't want to put you off in any way, but commitment is the watchword in our field so you need to be sure this is what you want."

It has all been so easy, Sam wondered as she left the council office what Christopher would say when he got back from work this evening. There was plenty of time before the course started and of course she would need to find a nursery for James. MacDonald's for lunch. Success, not so much for the junk food but for the small gift toy the cafe provided. After a spell on the swings in the park the two of them went back to the flat where James was soon engrossed in a cartoon on the box.

Sam was full of pleasurable expectation for the rest of the day. When she related the day's happenings to Christopher when he got back from work she felt her spirits dip as he welcomed her words with a frown. "Bloody hell Sam, how the hell do you expect us all to live on my income? Have you given that a tiny bit of thought? No more grants or loans now. We're in the real world and no mistake. As soon as our free accommodation ends we'll have to find somewhere to live for a start."

He was a miserable bugger bursting her bubble like that yet she had to admit that she hadn't really looked closely enough at the practicalities of her plans.

"Thank you very much for your support Kit. Well I'm not going to be shelf filling at Tesco to earn a few bob, that's for sure. Alright I should have asked about money. There may be grants, bursaries whatever. They're so desperate for people I'm sure there's some form of financial incentive. I'm going to fill in the application anyway, might take it back to the office tomorrow and ask about the finances." Sam was annoyed with herself for not considering the money but she was equally annoyed at her so-called partner for his complete lack of support in her endeavours with regard to a career. The look the two of them exchanged didn't augur well for a quite family evening.

Whether it was a peace offering or not Sam wasn't sure, but Christopher volunteered to put James to bed and read him a story. When he came back from the bedroom again Sam poured him a beer and offered a smile. The thin response she got was better than nothing was her take on the matter. "There's a few months to go before the autumn term starts so I'll look for some kind of job in the meantime."

Kit nodded, sipped his beer and started reading some paperwork he'd brought back from the office. "Starting a new job isn't easy you know Sam." Again she wasn't sure about him, was that some form of apology or what?

When Sam's mobile rang it was her mum on the line wanting to know how her grandson liked living in Kent. Of course Sam was pleased at the chance of talking to someone who might appreciate her news about the social work course starting in the autumn. Maggie was only too happy to join in Sam's enthusiasm at her prospects, although being the wise old bird she was she quickly came round to question of finance. "What does Christopher think about all that? Can you manage with regards to money while you're on that course?"

Sam glanced across at her partner, who was pretending not to listen, eyes glued to the television screen. "Bit of a shock but he'll come round, worried about money."

97

"Look here darling Trylon and I would be only too happy to help out with that."

Kit must have guessed that the conversation had come round to finance because he looked over at Sam, frowned and shook his head angrily.

"I'm going into that tomorrow Mum, seems like there are bursaries available and possibly maintenance loans."

Maggie clucked. "Don't want to get yourselves enmeshed in a lot of debt darling. As I said I'm sure we can help. Anyway that wasn't why I rang. We haven't seen James for a while and we both thought we might drop down to see you all in your new place. I know from what you've said that you can't put us up, but we could stay in a hotel and meet up for a few days."

"That would be lovely mum. James would love to see his grandma."

So it was all settled, or so Sam thought when she put the phone down, but she had reckoned without the sharp-eared Kit. When she glanced across at him she was met by another scowl. "You know starting a new job is pretty stressful Sam and here you are arranging family outings and discussing our financial affairs without so much as by your leave.

"For God sake Christopher it was my mum I was talking to not a stranger. She's interested in what her family are doing and whether she can help if needed. What's wrong with that?"

"Yes well, I'd rather we sorted out our own lives if you don't mind." He was a good looking boy but frowns and scowls didn't suit him.

"We *are* sorting ourselves out but if it's all the same to you a I'd like a say in that sorting out." She was getting angry herself now. She didn't want a row and couldn't really understand where Christopher was coming from. It brought home to her the fact that although they'd lived together for quite a while now and had a son they both adored, there was something missing from their relationship, something of that intricate intimacy that should exist between lovers. She didn't analyse it in those terms yet she did wish for a little more empathy from her partner in life.

Kit switched off the television without asking Sam if she wanting to continue watching it, storming out of the room presumably to go to bed and sulk. Sam stayed at the table reading through the application form for the social services course. There was nothing in it that changed her mind so she filled in the details determined to take it back to the council offices in the morning. She would in the meantime look for a temporary job to fill in the time before the course started in the autumn.

Tired, she went upstairs to bed to find all the lights out and Christopher apparently fast asleep in the bed. She sighed inwardly at what she regarded as his disappointing reaction to her plans, went into the bathroom before considerately slipping under the duvet so as not to wake her sleeping partner. But he wasn't asleep and as soon as Sam settled down he moved ponderously across to her side of the bed, his intentions obvious.

"No Christopher, not tonight, I'm whacked out. I just want to go to sleep." After a few more attempts at amorous persuasion he turned away with a muttered, "Fuck you then" and left her to quickly fall into a dreamless sleep.

Chapter 12

"Well dad I am convinced it's what I want to do, and, anyway, I've signed, and delivered my entry forms now."

"I get the impression that Christopher isn't over the moon with your plans."

Maggie looked worried. James fidgeted impatiently. "How are things between you two anyway, any plans for tying the knot?"

Trylon and Maggie were at the flat to take James out to Howletts Wild Animal Park where, so the advertisements said, there was large herd of elephants. James had always been fascinated by the giant creatures ever since seeing them in his picture books but had never seen one live until now. Sam was going with them relishing the thought of a day out in the warm sunshine. It was going to be an early summer by all accounts.

Later, as she watched James sitting on his grandfather's shoulders laughing like a banshee, she couldn't stop her thoughts drifting back to her relationship with Christopher Malpas. When they had first met in the early days at university she had fallen for him in a big way but then came pregnancy followed by his horrified reaction to it. Alright he had accepted his responsibilities and they had made something of a life together yet the magic of the first days had gone and now, well now, she really didn't know. One thing was certain and that was that she must make her own life whatever happened between her and the father of her child from now on.

Trylon interrupted her chain of thought. "Sam I think this young man needs a change of pants."

She took her child into the toilets to do the necessary. Then they all settled down on a bench in the sunshine to eat ice-creams – another need for a clean-up, this time at the other end of the excited child. Oh the joys of motherhood yet she saw the huge compensations when James put his arms round her neck and kissed her. "Love elephants," he said, his bright smile making it all worthwhile.

Chapter 13

"Not for a minute would I even try to limit you access to James."

"That's what you say now but once this Steven bloke is on the scene permanently what will happen then?"

She thought Christopher was being unreasonably angry. When she looked at him now there was no stirring of emotion. What had once been had gone forever. Yet with a touch of prurience she did remember that slender boyish body that she had once so lusted after.

"I'm not having James call him 'dad' that's for sure."

"No one's even considered that."

Sam felt like she was being interrogated and all because she and her lover Steven Bradbury had decided to move in together. Actually the move was to Steven's flat as that was rather larger than hers. Christopher had known about their relationship for months and until now had accepted as a normal progression in their separated lives.

"Where's the boy now?" He still sounded angry even after drinking the mug of tea Sam had given him.

Sam sighed. "He's at school of course, where did you think he was at lunch time on a Wednesday?"

"Yes well. Remember I didn't have the pleasures of taking him there for his first day not like some."

"You could have come with us; you said you had a meeting that day. All a matter of priorities isn't it?"

"I have to work, you know that particular day I couldn't get away. You know that bloody well."

"I'm not accusing you of anything, just pointing out the facts."

When things between her and Christopher had declined to an unpleasant level of constant bickering Sam had moved to a tiny flat in Faversham to be near her coursework. She had a bursary and a no interest maintenance loan while Christopher paid her some money for James's upkeep so she could just about get by. She soon began to appreciate her new home and the surrounding countryside. The old buildings, the proximity to the sea and the interesting shops made Faversham a delight to live in. She read somewhere that it had been mentioned in the Domesday Book.

That was all before she'd even met Steven Bradbury, an established social worker picked to provide mentoring to her as she neared the end of her two years of training. The fact that it wasn't long before they became lovers was very definitely not what the powers that be meant by mentoring, but when you're in love to hell with the rules. The relationship had worked well so far. James liked Steven and although he remained loyal to Christopher as his real dad he appreciated being spoiled by the man he called uncle Steven.

Sam loved the work she was doing although some of the harrowing cases she came across did cause her to worry finding her emotions engaged to an unsustainable degree. At first she had worked as part of a team with Steven as the lead partner. Now, after a year in the job, she was on her own as far as the work in the field was

103

concerned although there was always support and reassurance back in the office.

During this time Christopher had kept in touch and once or twice had made a play to rekindle what had once been a loving relationship. Sam had rejected the idea even before her thing with Steven had developed. They'd given it a go was her view and sadly it hadn't worked out so what was the point of trying to resurrect a failed relationship. That was despite the rather desperate attempts by Kit to change her mind.

Then there was Steven whose thoughtful mentoring had given her the confidence to go about dealing with some pretty harrowing cases while keeping herself objective. Then when the stresses of the day were calmed to try and put her work to one side and relax with James who found life something to enjoy. Sam shared in her little boy's eagerness to engage in adventure. When she first brought Steven back to the flat for a cup of tea, the two of them hit it off straight away. Her mentor was only a few years older than Sam but was by the time she met him a seasoned social worker. He was tall and willowy with a shock of fair hair that refused to accept instruction and a smile was never far from his lips.

Over the months when Sam and Steven had attended cases together, they became close almost by accident, enjoying each other's company on a friendly basis until one day when Sam had been deeply affected by the removal of a child from his mother and failed to keep her emotions under control. It was then that Steven took her in his arms for what started out as an avuncular embrace and ended in something distinctly more passionate. They waited until Sam finished her course before she agreed to move in with him and from there on in the three of them lived in harmony although Christopher wasn't at all happy about the arrangement.

James on the other hand was happy to be spoiled by his Uncle Steven and by his father on those occasions when he deigned to turn up to take him out. He might not have understood the ramifications of adult relationships but as long as people were kind to him that was all that mattered. And to the young boy life was exciting full of new things to discover. He liked school, liked the other children in his class. James was a happy boy.

It was the evening after a visit from her ex-partner. "So what did Christopher Malpas want then?"

"Oh just the usual. Unhappy about us living together and losing his son as he described it."

There was a frown on the young man's usually cheerful face. "I thought we'd been through all that. The boy's not calling me Dad and Kit can have all the access he wants or at least what you deem to be reasonable. Not trying for a comeback is he?"

Sam laughed. "No not any more; he's given up on that I'm sure." She massaged the back of her lover's neck and quietly whispered in his ear. "And even if he hadn't he wouldn't stand a chance against you lover."

Steven relaxed, "Anything to eat in this flat?"

"I might find something if I try really hard. Tell you what you sit there, I'll get you a beer out of the fridge and while you're drinking it I'll rustle up a three course meal."

Steven sat back in his chair, closed his eyes and murmured. "One course will do darling."

He was tired, sitting there wondering why he put himself through all the hassle every single day yet he was happy. Happy to have found Sam, and of course young James. He could put up with the strains and stresses of work as long as he has Sam to come home to. As he sat there it came to him that between them there were some decisions to make. He loved James like his own but that didn't stop him wanting kids of his own. They hadn't discussed the matter yet. Maybe tonight was the night for revealing his longing. He still hesitated. Sam had her lovely boy. Perhaps she was satisfied with what she had. It seemed strange to him that evening that despite their easy intimacy they had never broached the subject before.

Chapter 14

Take as much time as you need they'd said, not that Sam had been listening. There was no meaning in her life now, no reason to think rationally, no reason to do anything but weep her heart out and that in itself was exhausting in the extreme. Even the gentle Steven couldn't find a way through to help her overwhelming grief. The vision of her tear stained face haunted him as did his inability to provide succour to the stricken woman. He took two compassionate days off to sit with Sam, yet he might as well have been on Mars for all the good it did.

For Sam life had stopped. People talked about time being a great healer, yet for Sam time didn't heal anything; it was just a measure of the blackness that invaded her every thought. She had no idea of how she had got through the funeral. Half supported by Steven and with Maggie and Trylon in grief stricken attendance, she had endured the ritual in a dark cloud with little comprehension of what was going on around her. She had fought off the selfish anger from Christopher Malpas. Anger she felt justified as guilt struck her like blows to the heart. Now, the hideous autopsy behind her, and a small urn of ashes on her dressing table, that was all she had left of that vibrant young boy who had been her darling James.

"You want something to eat sweetheart?"

Sam shook her head. She hadn't eaten much at all since the accident. Steven worried she was starving herself to death. "I know my words won't help, but you have to carry on, you have to try and get some food inside you."

"Just get me a large gin please Steven, then stop fussing about me like a headless chicken." She glared at her partner if that's what he still was. After the initial period following James's death, when she had welcomed his enfolding arms, she had refused to let him touch her at all.

Steven could see only too well the effect of days of mourning on the face of the young women he loved. Haggard was the word, pale as death itself, hair unruly and unclean. Misery etched deeply in her features.

"You know, Steven, I will eventually get over James's accident, I just need time." She knew he was doing his best. Now she offered a weak smile in his direction, a small recognition of his caring attention. Neither of them realised it but that evening was a turning point in Sam's grief. That night she slept for the whole night, waking to the same horrible remembrance, but *that* day with a new acceptance that life must go on. She showered, put on a new sweat shirt and jeans, before eating three slices of toast and peanut butter.

"You can tell them I'm coming back to work tomorrow Steven."

"I think you should take their offer of counselling first sweetie."

"Fuck counselling. I already know the phrases and cliches they would trot out, and they're not for me thank you very much."

"They may make in a condition."

"In that case they'll have lost a social worker and bearing in mind the work load I think perhaps they might make an exception to the rules, don't you?" She smiled a smile that was very nearly the old Sam. Steven felt his spirits rise at that welcome sight going off to work with what might be described as joy in his heart, a new feeling of hope, hope that he might yet get back the young woman he loved so much.

The next day Sam drove her old Mini back to the familiar office to take whatever they threw at her. To absorb herself in other's people's problems might just enable her to put her own misery into perspective or at least that's what she hoped. Carl Rocklove, her team leader, quietly asked her to come and have chat in his office.

"What can I say love." He pursed his lips and sighed.

"There's no point in saying anything more Carl. I just want to get back to the job. I can promise you whatever my inner thoughts I will be able to do that job." She raised a weak smile, a smile that had cost her to produce, but a smile that she would have be using later in the day when she came up against whatever case was allocated to her.

Sam did get through her day. The cases she had worked on were probably particularly chosen by Carl as soft cases, but nevertheless she did get through them without making a fool of herself .By the evening she felt better, if desperately tired.

"What about a dog?" Steven asked out of the blue. "I know where there's one going free of charge."

Sam fixed him with angry stare. "You think a dog will compensate for the loss of a child do you?"

In fact Steven hadn't for a moment thought that, but now he could at once see how tactless his suggestion had been. "No sorry love, thoughtless of me, just came across this little Jack Russell being consigned to a kennels and thought we, you, might like a dog around the place."

Suddenly the idea of an animal in the flat didn't seem all that alien to her thoughts. "But we're out all day and that wouldn't be fair on the poor creature, would it?"

"Tommy isn't a puppy and his present owner tells me he's used to being left during the day so that wouldn't be a problem." He shrugged his shoulders. "Just a thought."

Her first day back at work and Steven comes up with this dog thing. Her body felt like lead, perhaps she was just tired, perhaps things would lighten in her mind as times passed. No it wouldn't was her next thought. How could one ever get over the loss of a child, it was impossible to imagine that possibility. She would live in this state of half-life forever. The depression, lifted a little by her day at work, now returned with full intensity. The tears came in abundance soaking Steven's shirt as she clung to him in desperate despair.

"Not sure you should have gone back to work so soon sweetheart." Steven was desperate to find ways of lifting Sam's spirits, desperate to have the old Sam back while at the same timed recognising that wouldn't happen for some time to come. He stroked her hair, kissed the top of her head, held her tight.

"How about fish and chips?"

Sam laughed quietly. "You and your stomach, food a priority whatever the situation." It was meant as light-hearted teasing and it worked.

"Yes, go on, get your fish and chips." It came to her then that despite her feelings of desolation she was suddenly very hungry, maybe a good sign she hoped. She loved Steven and hated the trauma she imposed on him day after day. He was a good man and she was lucky to have him.

For some time, and long before the tragedy, it had been in Steven's mind to suggest to Sam that they should try for their own baby. He had loved James and missed him terribly, yet the question of their own child, his and Sam's still lingered in his thoughts. Now waiting in the queue at the fish and chip shop, he was thinking about that unborn child again. To suggest it now would look like he was offering a palliative for the loss of Sam's beloved boy. He knew nothing could replace the boy but that shouldn't mean that there shouldn't be another child in Sam's and his life. Timing was all. How much healing time would be needed before he could raise such a delicate subject he wondered as he paid for the cardboard box handed to him by the man behind the counter?

Chapter 15

They were right of course. Time did heal or at least form a scab over the wound so it didn't hurt so much. Now the thought of a few days away in France brought a frisson of excitement to her mind. She would never forget James of course, but maybe she could learn to live with the emptiness, move on to filling the gap with other worthwhile things.

They took the ferry from Dover and drove for hours to reach their destination which was a small gite in a village quite near to Bordeaux. It was a ridiculously long journey of over 500 miles but they shared the driving and the prospect of a few days of absolute relaxation in the sunshine kept them going. Arriving in the village and following instructions they were welcomed by a wizened old lady dressed all in black who was the custodian of the key to their gite.

The lady in black introduced herself as Madame Laboise. She insisted that they take a glass of anisette with her to welcome them to France and to her village. Once the old lady had done her duty and gone back to her own home, they decided to look for a bistro to eat that evening and to leave shopping for food until the next day. They were both shattered, but sitting outside the bistro in the still warm evening air, eating veal cutlets and drinking glasses of Medoc wine, they felt relaxed and, what was more to the point, happy in each other's company. It was almost as though they had only recently met and were getting to know each other for the first time. The trauma over James's death was fading. The wall of grief that had separated them for a while was crumbling. Sam was so grateful to Steven for his caring patience over the last months. She felt she had never really thanked him for his gentle consideration throughout her misery. Now that was in the past and although the sadness would remain probably forever, she wanted to renew her love for Steven and prove to him that his faithful perseverance was lovingly appreciated.

That night in the big rather saggy old bed provided by the gite they made quiet love before dropping off to contented sleep. For some reason Sam woke in the middle of the night to find the bed beside her empty. She looked across to the window to see Steven standing there looking out onto a moonlit garden. Slipping quietly from under the duvet she crept across the room to put her arms around her partner from behind.

"What's up love?"

Steven produced a small sound in his throat that might just have been a chuckle. "Nothing really, the bright moonlight woke me up drawing me over to the window. Then I got to thinking about our lives together and whether...." He stopped talking.

"And whether what?"

He again hesitated. Then with a rush. "Well hell if you must know. Whether we'd ever have a family of our own. Sorry love but I can't help my thoughts can I?"

It was a climactic moment. She tightened her hold on the man who had gently guided her through the worst trauma a mother could ever endure. She loved the man and knew very well that what he was asking was very reasonable. Most loving couples wanted children so why should they be any different. She would always love James but there was room in her heart for more love and that could perhaps be bestowed on another child, a child fathered by the lovely man now gripped tightly in her arms.

"We can try. No guarantees in these things Steven, are there?"

He turned to face her and they clung together in an embrace that confirmed their future together at least as far as having a family was concerned. Back in the saggy old bed neither slept for a while but lying quietly, their bodies still entwined, each with their own seething thoughts.

The next day dawned bright and sunny and despite having no food they stayed in bed revelling in the holiday spirit, the sense of adventure and the absolute delight of being able to do whatever they felt like once they decided to emerge from their cocoon. Then there was a knock on the door. Steven scrambled to put on his dressing gown to venture down to find out who was visiting so early. There on the step was Madame Laboise holding two long baguettes and a bag ofomething else.

In fractured English she said that they must be hungry and she has brought food for their breakfast knowing that they probably hadn't done any shopping as yet. Steven voiced his thanks in schoolboy French and offered Madame money to pay for the food but she waved it away. More than that he understood that they were invited to an open-air party to be held in a nearby park the next evening. Who said the French didn't like the English Steven said as he explained to Sam what the old lady had wanted. The bread was still warm, the butter firm and delicious and the strawberry jam was to die for. If this was the start of their holiday then it was going to be the trip of their lives.

Paradise nearly evaporated however when they arrived in the park for the party to which Madame Laboise had invited them to. It turned out to be very much a family affair with kids chasing each other round amongst the trees. They were greeted with smiling faces and made very welcome. The local wine they were offered was excellent, the food to die for and the two Englishers were enjoying themselves in the warm evening sunshine when Steven, chatting to a local man who identified himself as Jacques, got a nasty shock. Jacques spoke reasonably good English and when Steven asked him what the party they were enjoying was for. His new friend explained that about a year ago a local eight-year old lad had drowned in the river. Now the distraught mother had announced she was pregnant again. The party was a celebration of life continuing through sadness into light and new birth.

"We've paid our respects love, should we make a move?" He was only too aware that if Sam found out why they were indulging themselves in these pleasant surroundings she was likely to be very upset.

"Why on earth should we leave now, it's only early and I'm enjoying myself."

"Just thought you might be tired that's all."

"Come off it, that's not the reason, is it? Not because of the reason for this party is it lover? I know all about that boy who died and I think it's a lovely thought that someone can lovingly move on after what I'm sure was a horrible period of grief. You thought I'd be upset because of me losing James just like the French mother did a year ago, didn't you? And yet last night we agreed to try for a child of our own so shouldn't that have told you that like Louise I'm ready to move on?" She kissed him gently on the mouth while the French party-goers around them smiled indulgently.

They didn't leave the party then. Instead they stayed enjoying the atmosphere and the local wine until near on midnight. When, walking arm in arm, they did eventually return to the gite it was in a spirit of release and possibilities. A corner had been turned last night and this evening that had been confirmed as the way to go.

The rest of their short stay was taken up with strolls round the beautiful port city of Bordeaux, visits to the Cite du Vin, the cathedral, the Mirror d'Eau interchanged with stop offs at pavement cafes and tasting of various recommended wines. They bought a couple of cases of Bergerac to take back home. That was all lovely but what Sam enjoyed most was her new mind set, the excitement of their joint decision to go for a baby. Everything else faded into insignificance compared to that possibility.

They got home on a rainy Sunday evening which contrasted dramatically with the few days sunshine they'd experienced in France. Nevertheless it was always good to be home no matter how enjoyable the holiday.

Chapter 16

Sam had been looking forward to her first day back in the office after the trip to France. There'd been an email on her computer asking her report to Carl Rocklove on Monday morning. She expected that at that meeting she would be told that she was now ready to deal with more complicated cases on her own without a back-up person with her.

In the event her expectations were confirmed. "Good holiday Sam?"

Carl was a tall gangly man with a permanently worried expression on his face, but then when he smiled it was like the sun coming out from behind the clouds. Then anyone could see the warmth and caring personality that motivated the man. Today he was already smiling across his desk at an expectant Sam.

"It was great but I'm here now and ready to go."

"That's the spirit. I'm cutting you loose from now on to work on your own with the very worst cases that are thrown at us but listen to me Sam. This is serious stuff and for the next month I want to have a personal chat with you about every case you're handling. I know it sounds like nurse-maiding but experience is all you know so I hope you'll take in the spirit intended. Anyway congratulations." He reached across the desk to shake her by the hand. "I'm quite confident that you're up to the task Sam."

That task that Carl had referred to involved a single mother about whom anonymous reports had filtered in of possible child neglect. Sam knew she wouldn't be expected, that she might have difficulty even getting through the door but that was where her training came in or at least she hoped it was. She climbed the stairs to the third floor of the tower block, the lift not working that morning before knocking on the door on number fifty seven. A harassed looking woman half opened the door and peered out.

"If it's about the rent I already told that bitch on the phone that she couldn't get blood out of a stone."

"No Mrs. Wallace it's not about the rent. I'm with social services. I just wanted a chat to see how you were getting on."

"Oh great. I'm on your list for social visiting am I? More like some nosey-parker has grassed me up, said I'm not looking after my kids properly. So you can just fuck off and leave us in peace. My kids are fine thank you very much." The door slammed shut with what seemed like finality.

Sam knocked again, this time with no response. She waited a few minutes and knocked again. This time the door opened to reveal the same tear stained face that had appeared the first time around. "You better come in then. I know your lot are persistent buggers they are so I might as well get it over with."

Sam edged through the door to find what she'd expected, a room in chaos with food remains, broken toys and bits of paper strewn about. There was a girl child clinging to her mother's dress and a little boy playing with a toy car on the concrete floor in the far corner and she could hear the plaintive cries of a baby from another room.

The two children she could see appeared to be reasonably healthy with no signs of physical abuse but Sam was well aware what she could see at first sight may just be the tip of the iceberg.

"Mrs. Wallace," Sam smiled, trying to appear friendly. "I'm here to help not to criticise, but I'm sure you'll understand that if we get a call about a situation we have to follow it up. What are these two called?"

"This here is Maisie and the lad is Bobby and the one making all that bloody noise is Tammy. They're good kids really but it's difficult to look after three young ones at the same time you know." She reached for a packet of cigarettes before lighting up with a slightly guilty look on her face and inhaling deeply.

"Expensive these days aren't they," Sam smiled again.

Truth was that the children showed no signs of bruising or other physical hurt. True they were a trifle grubby but not unhappy as far as she could see.

"I could get help for you if you wanted to give up smoking." She remembered her training not to be judgemental, not to coerce people into doing something which was right but which the client resisted.

Mrs. Wallace blew out her cheeks. "Helps me cope with these three, chucks." She sighed. "I know I should and the cost is something terrible."

"Look Mrs. Wallace."

The mother was relaxing now, any perceived threat from authority had diminished to almost zero. "Call me Doris, love."

"Alright Doris it is. What about it then, shall I make an appointment for you with the local Stop Smoking Service. What have you got to lose?"

"Well I'll give it a go if I can get someone to look after the baby. I could go on the day when these two are at nursery"

Sam left the very basic flat in the nondescript block feeling rather pleased with herself. What was more important she wasn't going to have to recommend to her boss anything that might involve separating a mother from her children. Back home that evening her ebullient mood continued. As soon as Steven got through the door he was somewhat taken aback by the warmth of her greeting as she flung her arms around him and kissed him in an unbridled way that nearly knocked him off he is feet.

Chapter 17

Quite naturally Sam took a Boots pregnancy test before telling Steven she thought he was going to be a father. However something inside her had already indicated a change in bodily metabolism so she wasn't at all surprised with the positive result. They had both been hoping for such an outcome ever since that decision made back in France in the Summer. However there was something that Sam didn't tell Steven and that was a weird feeling of guilt towards her dead son James. Would he be upset that she was going to have another child, a child that might usurp the love she had for her lost boy. In her mind she promised James that he would always be in her thoughts and her love whatever children she might have in the future. In the end of all that soul searching she concluded that her lost son, with his caring and generous spirit, would have wanted his mother to go on and have other children.

Now excited rather than unsettled, she visited the local surgery in due course to have the Boots test confirmed much to her own and Steven's delight.

"Let's get married shall we?" Was almost the first thing that Steven said when he heard the confirmation of her good news.

Sam looked at him for a long moment before falling into his arms, tears flowing freely down her cheeks. When she finally recovered something like her normal equilibrium all she could say was, "I love you Steven Bradbury."

They did decide to tie the knot. "The child might find having Mr. and Mrs. Bradbury as their mum and dad less confusing than having Ms. Sam Makepeace and Mr. Steven Bradbury, don't you think?"

They visited the local Registry Office to fix a date. A small affair, they agreed. Of course Trylon and Maggie and grandma Grace on her side would be invited. Steven would invite his mum, his father had died young a few years ago, and his brother Michael who worked and lived in Brussels. Then it was down to friends. The only one of her friends from Uni Sam had kept in touch with was Jemma Smith so she rang her to tell her the news and invite her down with her new husband Dougie. They both wanted Carl Rocklove there with his long standing partner Mellie. He has been very supportive to both of them in recent times. Sam thought back to her earlier life when the gentle Jason had kept her going at a difficult period in her life, but then the time distance was too great so no, not Jason. Christopher Malpas? Should she ask the father of her lost child? After all they had once been close and parented James together. He had done well at D.S.Smith and was already a section leader whatever that was.

"So what about Kit Malpas?"

She saw Steven's creased brow. "Not if you don't want Steven, I just thought."

He shrugged. "Fine if you want and if he'll come, you know what he's like."

When Sam had been checked over by the doctor he told her she was about six weeks along with her pregnancy and gave her an estimated date in July next year as the date of birth. It was an exciting time and although memories of James kept coming into her mind, she still felt joy with both her impending marriage and next year's birth.

The day of the wedding dawned dark and gloomy, rain clouds threatening, very cold after an early morning frost. Sam woke to find Steven already out of bed and offering her a cup of tea which she gratefully accepted. He kissed her on the forehead.

"Ready for your big day? Perhaps we should have gone for a church wedding with all the trimmings. I know you women like that sort of thing. Sam I hope you aren't too disappointed."

She reached up and pulled him down on top of her. "Of course not you big oaf. I'm marrying the man I love and all my friends and family will be there, what's there to be disappointed about."

Three hours later with all those family and friends gathered for the Registry Office ceremony they were part of a happy group of people. Sam wore a deep blue velvet dress and had even managed a cheeky little hat. Every one clapped and cheered when the Registrar pronounced them man and wife. They kissed sedately before being swamped by well-wishers wanting to kiss, hug them or shake their hands. Jemma hugged Sam in her arms in a display of affection that quite took her breath away. Everyone wanted to get in on the act of wishing the young couple a lifetime of happiness. Grandma Grace was crying her eyes out. Maggie singled out Miranda, Steven's mother to ensure she didn't feel out of it. Michael got talking to Kit Malpas and no doubt bringing him to date with the history between him and Sam.

The pub where they'd booked a private room was only just down the road so the whole party trailed down to the Pig and Whistle to enjoy the wedding breakfast. Everyone invited had turned up even including that certain Christopher Malpas.

"You look great Sam." He smiled as he kissed her on the cheek. "Congratulations, I'm very pleased for you." He hesitated before adding somewhat wistfully, "This might have been us Sam if things had turned out differently."

Sam smiled and moved away without replying.

After the toasts and good wishes for the married couple, Trylon took Sam on one side.

"Look love, Grandma Grace, Maggie and me got together and decided the best thing we could do for you and Steven as a present to mark the occasion was to give you the money for a deposit on a house of your own, always assuming the two of you can afford to pay the monthly instalments on a mortgage." He thrust an envelope into her hands. "With all our love and best wishes for that baby when it arrives next year."

Sam had opened the envelope and looked inside. "We can't accept this Dad it's far too much, and even if I did I'm sure Steven would have something to say about it."

The offer was put on one side for the time being. As Sam drank her champagne she looked round the table at the people she loved and those she hoped she would grow to love once she got to know them and her heart was full. She might almost have said that 'her cup runneth over.'

The newly married couple planned to spend their first night at home in their flat before flying off from Southend airport next morning for a week in Ibiza. They weren't expecting blazing sunshine, December being one of the coldest months in the resort, but on the other hand it was warm compared to the frosts and cold winds that England had on offer.

Chapter 18

Honeymoon a pleasant memory, Christmas. spent happily across country with Trylon and Maggie. Now in the harsh reality of January Saturday morning lying in a warm bed sipping tea, Sam raised the question of houses. Steven had been reluctant to accept the deposit money from Sam's parents and grandmother. Now from the pleasant proximity to the woman he loved, he again voiced his opposition to buying a house with the help of the Makepeace deposit money.

"It's a bit late to think of turning it down now weeks after the gift was made Steven." Sam couldn't for the life of her see why her husband should be so reluctant to accept the money; money given with all the good intentions and indeed love in the world.

Steven sighed. "It's all too easy. I feel we should save for the deposit ourselves. All those poor buggers I come across everyday living in their crummy flats. They'll never but never have a home of their own and here we are being offered one on a plate as it were."

Sam snuggled close and kissed her lover firmly on the mouth. "You're just an old puritan at heart sweety, but I'm not, so there. You should give some thought to what you poor wife wants don't you think?"

Puritan or not it was some time later before they got back to the subject of houses by which time Steven appeared to have relaxed his attitude towards buying a house helped by the generous family windfall.

"I suppose it wouldn't do any harm to look around, see what's on the market."

Sam gave him another kiss. "Just for that I'll get up and cook you bacon and eggs you beautiful man."

She was as good as her word and by the time Steven had showered and dressed in his weekend casuals there was breakfast waiting on the kitchen table, the scrubbed pine table they'd picked up for a song from a local magazine advert. That table had always been the site for serious discussions in the past and was now this Saturday morning was to be so again.

They decided once Sam had showered and dressed in warm clothes to make a tour of the town to see what local estate agents had to offer. The cold was bitter that morning seeming to reach inside to chill the very marrow of their bones while their hot breath condensed in the cold air as they walked, Despite the cold Sam had a warm feeling inside her as they walked arm in arm down the high street, calling into agents to collect brochures for houses they thought they might be able to afford the mortgage on.

Exciting maybe but damn confusing with the variations on offer. It was a buyers' market the agents said encouragingly with friendly offers for them to view any properties in which they might be interested. By one o'clock they'd had quite enough for one day so settled on the Pig and Whistle for lunch and a pint of beer. The landlord recognised them and welcomed them like old friends. There was an open fire in the main room and they settled down to enjoy their hot pasties and good ale in a spirit of contentment. Sam in particular was pleased with her morning's work in persuading Steven that looking for a house was not breaching any tenets of his social responsibility. She loved the man with all her heart but boy he could be a bit straight-laced at times when it came to things like their way of living so today was a victory even if a soft one.

Steven took a great gulp of his beer, frowned, picked up the pile of brochures and let them drop down on the table in front of them. "What on earth do we want all this shit for Sam? What's wrong with what we've got?"

Sam edged up to the disgruntled man at her side. She felt like sighing too, but kept it back. Instead saying quietly. "Well for a start this one might appreciate a garden to play in." She rubbed her belly and smiled up at Steven determined to keep the peace. In fact she'd found the morning exciting with all its possibilities and she couldn't wait to take a closer look at the brochures now scattered about in front of them.

"Kids accept whatever situation they're born into" is what he said, but Sam could tell the mention of children had softened her husband's viewpoint. She leant over and whispered in his ear. "Shall we finish our beer and then go home to bed for a quick nap."

That got the young man gulping down his ale, collecting the brochures together, putting on his jacket, ready to leave as soon as Sam was ready. Later safe in their warm flat he did deign to look at the paperwork they'd collected from the estate agents that morning and began to show some interest in what was on offer. They had a good idea of what they could afford so discarded straight away the properties outside their price range. That still left quite a few for them to consider whether they wanted to view them. "Wrong time of year to be looking at houses," Steven grumbled.

127

"Oh stop being such a misery guts. If they look acceptable in January they're going to be great when spring comes."

Some common sense from Sam led them to adopting an approach of reducing the number of brochures by eliminating all those that were out of their price range or obviously unsuitable and throwing them in the bin. By dinner time they were down to three or four promising properties, three very much in suburbia and one a bit further out of town. They both had holiday owing so determined to ask for a couple of days off at the back end of the coming week to give them time to start looking at houses. Sam felt the day had been worthwhile and while Steven grumbled at the possible upheaval to their joint life she could tell he was becoming more on board with the idea of a new home by the hour.

Thursday, the day they'd designated as house-hunting day, dawned grim and January-like with a harrowing wind, scudding clouds and a bone chilling cold in the air. Nothing daunted, they set out to complete the time table scheduled with agents and house owners. They saw two houses in the morning, both three bedroomed semi-detached suburban house with OK gardens Comfortable but to Sam's mind not what she wanted for her family home. Then back to the old Pig and Whistle again for a quick sandwich and half a pint of beer. They were becoming regulars the landlord joked.

After lunch they saw another property very similar to those seen that morning and then they drove towards Badlesmere in the heart of rural Kent where their final viewing of the day was to be found on the outskirts of the village. Sam immediately fell in love with the slate-roofed cottage and that was before she'd even been through the front door. Steven was shaking his head, probably at the thought of being stuck out in the wilds of the countryside. Nevertheless he rang the bell, waiting to be welcomed by Mr. And Mrs. Colthorpe. The couple were both in their eighties and explained they were moving to be nearer their daughter who lived in Coggeshall in Essex. They couldn't have been kinder, insisting on their visitors sitting down for a cup of tea before showing them round their home. Once they got down to the purpose of their visit the interior of the cottage lived up to Sam's first impression. There were beams, an inglenook fireplace with a wood burner installed. The rooms were small but again, to Sam's way of thinking, characterful.

They thanked the Colthorpes and said they'd be in touch. Steven was on the way to the car when Mrs. Colthorpe took Sam by the arm and spoke quietly in her ear. "You're the kind of couple we would like to take over our lovely cottage. We've been so happy here and we would love to think of it going to people who would appreciate it, even love it. Shouldn't say this of course, Albert would kill me if he knew, but if you made an offer somewhere near the asking price I'm sure it would be accepted, but I think you should move quickly if that's what you want lovey."

They waved good bye before deciding to call in at the Falcon Inn before setting off for home. To get some idea of the area Sam said, although in reality she needed a gin to calm her excitement. Tact and careful reasoning were to be the order of the day from Sam's point of view. She mustn't let her excitement bubble over she told herself, although she did tell Steven what Mrs. Colthorpe had said to her as she was leaving the cottage.

"They want a quick sale Sam, don't fall for that one."

"You're just an old cynic Steven. No I really think she wants the place to go to someone she thinks will cherish it. Don't you like it then?"

"Very pretty, but would it be practical for us with a baby coming in July?" His lack of enthusiasm was already dampening Sam's delight at what she saw as a great find. Truth to say she'd already fallen in love with the place.

Sam decided to curb her enthusiasm for the time being, recognising that male stubbornness was entering the fray, if fray it was. She thought she knew how to deal with recalcitrant men even those she loved very dearly. So she changed the subject to work knowing that Steven would be happy to discuss particular cases in his folder despite having promised never to bring work home. While that was going on she poured him a whiskey and Canada dry and sat on his lap while he drank it. It was cosy inside the flat after the winter weather they'd experienced during their afternoon house hunting.

"Can we at least think about it overnight love? If you're really against the idea of the cottage we'll carry on looking at three bed-roomed semis in streets with houses all alike, and with no character at all." It was risky stepping up the rhetoric like that, but bloody hell she wanted that cottage even without roses round the door.

Steven frowned and shifting irritably in his chair. "Bloody hell Sam when you want something you're stubborn as a mule aren't you? And," he shook his head slowly from side to side, "you're prepared to use any old tactics to get your way."

"No lover I'm not. If in the morning you're still set against the idea I'll forget all about that damned cottage. What do you want for dinner?"

She left it at that, leaving her comfortable perch in Steven's his lap to go into the kitchen to prepare something to eat. She hummed as she scraped the potatoes, happy that her case had been made, knowing that her partner always hated disagreements between them. She thought there was a good chance of him coming round to her way of thinking particularly after what she planned for him when they were tucked in their warm bed for the night.

Breakfast that Saturday morning was a quiet affair. Sam was down first and started on the bacon and eggs while Steven took his time shaving and showering. When he did come into the kitchen and sat down at the table Sam immediately produced a fried breakfast which she placed in front of him like a magician producing a rabbit from a hat, poured him a mug of coffee and nudging a plate of toast in his direction.

"What's all this then, all part of the softening up process is it?" But he said it with a smile, a smile in which Sam sensed victory not that she would have used that word. After all they both had to be committed on a big decision like buying a house for instance. Steven made short work of the fry-up, finishing off with a couple of slices of toast and marmalade.

"I suppose I'll get no rest unless I agree to us making on offer for that damn place stuck out there in the wilds."

"No Steven it's not like that at all. If you're really against the idea that's fine, we'll look elsewhere."

Their eyes met, not so much a challenge more of a seeking out of the truth. "If we pitch the offer low perhaps they won't accept. I wouldn't place too much confidence on what the old bird said to you. She obviously wants to sell the place and..." he tailed off and pursed his lips.

"Well we'll see, but only if you want to go along with making an offer at all."

"I've said haven't I?"

131

Sam tucked her hair behind her left ear and in a tone that had a touch of weariness in it. "I'd be happier if you showed a touch more enthusiasm lover."

Steven shrugged but enough had been said for Sam to act. An offer wasn't a final commitment and if accepted perhaps Steven would come on board. There was no way she would want to go any further without Steven's compliance but it was a start and she felt good about that.

Was it all part of a plan or was it really just an off–the-cuff sort of thing. Anyway when Sam suggested they take a trip to Canterbury that Saturday Steven readily agreed. The fact that they would be going through Badlesmere on their way there and back was convenient, and it would have been ridiculous not to scout out the area for a property on which they were going to make an offer on come Monday morning or that's how it seemed to Sam.

On the short journey to Canterbury Steven was unexpectedly cheerful, chatting away to Sam about the baby due in a few months time. When they were in bed at night he loved to lie with his head on Sam's belly listening for sounds within her womb. If anything he was more excited by the coming birth than Sam herself. They were happy that morning each wanting to express their love by going along with whatever their partner wanted.

It was the first time Sam had visited the cathedral and like most people seeing it for the first time was overawed by its majestic splendour with its history of a murdered archbishop, slaughtered on the steps of his own alter at a king's whim. After that visit they spent the rest of their time exploring Canterbury's old town and then after a visit to a pub for a beer and a sandwich, went for a walk in Blean Woods, a National Nature Reserve. They both enjoyed walking, and had talked about getting a dog but then thought it would be unfair on the animal to be shut up all day while they were both at work so had decided against for the time being at least.

It was Steven who suggested they take another look at Matchstick Cottage on the way back, not to go inside but look at it from outside and get an idea of the neighbourhood. "We forgot to ask the Colthorpes about that strange name didn't we?"

"You could always rename it once it was ours."

"Stop the car." As soon as Steven pulled to a halt she leant across to kiss him lavishly on the lips.

"I really do love you, you stubborn old bugger, "she said once she'd got her breath back.

The cold meant nothing to that happy young couple that day. There was warmth enough between them to keep a regiment warm.

So it was come Monday morning, and with Steven's endorsement, Sam rang the agents and made the agreed offer.

"So sorry love," said an anonymous voice at the other end of the line, "you've been beaten to it. We've had another offer not half an hour ago which is higher than yours."

A deflated Sam rang Steven on his mobile to tell him the news. They had thought it was a done deed seeing the friendly reception they'd received from the Colthorpes.

"Should we make a higher offer, do you think?"

There was silence for a moment at the other end of the line. Steven didn't sigh or not that she heard, but she could imagine him doing that all the same.

"Look love I know how much you want that place so, yes, go ahead and offer another couple of thousand but that's it. We don't want to enter into a bidding war do we?"

Sam was on the phone to the agents straight away.

133

"So glad you rang Mrs. Bradbury, I was just going to call you. I've spoken to Mrs. Colthorpe and for some unaccountable reason they've decided to take your lower offer for the cottage," She paused, and Sam thought she could just see her shaking her head. "So it's all yours if you still want it."

Chapter 19

There hadn't been any trouble getting a mortgage with the Halifax, just a question of a survey. Their two incomes and the deposit money they'd received as a wedding present put them in a strong position but then there was all the paperwork to do at the solicitors. Conveyancing was a nightmare, energy performance certificates, stamp duty, deposits, contracts to be signed. All that with a vendor who was only too happy to oblige in making the transaction as painless as possible.

They went back to Matchstick Cottage while all this was going on to thank the Colthorpes for their marvellous help with buying the home.

"We wanted it to go to someone who would love it as much as we have dear. and you two seemed to be the couple who would do that" Mable Colthorpe explained, a tear or two running down her cheek. "When's the baby due sweetie?"

In fact they hadn't said a word about any babies, but there you are the question was asked. Sam looked across at Stephen, raising her eyebrows and smiling.

"Not until July Mrs. Colthorpe."

"That'll be lovely, warm weather then I should hope, and you'll be well settled in by that time if those damn solicitors get a move on that is. Would you care for another cup and a slice of this plum cake?"

They never saw the Colthorpes again but always remembered them with a sense of affection and indeed gratitude. They moved to Matchstick Cottage on a rainy day in the middle of February. They hired a van and with the help of Fred Norway moved their stuff out of the flat and into the cottage. It looked rather bare at first but Sam at least loved it from the start as she knew she would. Now they had three bedrooms and an extra small room downstairs that Mr. Colthorpe had called his study. The furniture from Steven's flat didn't really fill the place out so they would need to go to a few sales for some extra sticks of furniture.

After a glass of beer Fred had gone to take the van back to the hiring place. Sam and Steven left on their own felt rather strange in their new surroundings. It wasn't the sort of day for exploring outside so they lit the log-burner in living room, made themselves comfortable in front of that with a life-giving cup of tea and tried to absorb the atmosphere of their new home. Despite the rain lashing at the curtainless windows it was soon comfortable inside the cottage with the central heating adding to the warmth from the fire.

"Well lover what do you think?"

"I think we'll be very happy here, but what about you and all your doubts Steven?"

"If you're happy sweetheart then I'm happy. I'll be happier still when we get some curtains up and the whole place has been aired out."

Their happy reveries were interrupted by a knock on the door. Sam reluctantly got to her feet to see who the hell could be calling on a night like this. On the door step was a tall thin woman with wild grey hair carrying a box.

Before Sam could utter a word the visitor pressed forward giving Sam no option but to let her pass by her into the hallway.

"Mrs. Dalgetty, Agnes Dalgetty. I've brought you a cake, sort of welcome to the village you might say."

Sam took a deep breath. "Very kind of you Mrs. Dalgetty, but goodness me you shouldn't have come out on a night like this?"

"Saw the moving van didn't I? We loved Mable and Ronald and any one they sold Matchstick Cottage to must be alright people so I thought, well I thought, well you know, a cake."

Sam, now more in control of the situation, asked the windswept women to come into the living room to meet her husband which she did in a flurry of flying coats and bustling enthusiasm, during the course of which she managed to hand over the box presumably containing the promised cake.

"You'll stop for a cup of tea Mrs. Dalgetty?"

"Very kind, knew you would be the right sort of people, told Mason so, didn't I?" She dragged off the heavy overcoat she was wearing dropping it on the floor by the side of chair where she had comfortably lodged herself before leaning forward to warm her hands on the fire which was now burning brightly. Steven, who up to now had not said a word, enquired where the Dalgettys lived and was told.

"We're you nearest neighbour but one." She sniffed and ran her hand through her unruly mob of damp hair. Your nearest, neighbour I mean won't be bringing a cake round I can tell you that for nothing." Her cackling laugh, Steven supposed, was telling them something about their nearest neighbour, but quite what that something was they had no idea. He was saved from asking the question by the return of Sam from the kitchen where she had managed to unearth a tray which she now carried with three mugs of tea and a plate with a cream sponge on it.

"Sugar Mrs. Dalgetty?"

"Agnes please, two spoons if I may, see you found the cake, hope you enjoy it."

Their visitor seemed rather restless, her eyes flicking round the room as if to see what these intruders had done to her friends' home, which wasn't a lot as they hadn't done much unpacking yet. Then as though someone had pressed a switch their visitor rose from her chair, picked up her coat, and hurried towards the front door murmuring "Mason will be wondering where I am, must go."

Before Sam could get to her feet to see the old lady out out she had the front door open and was off into the stormy night leaving behind her an untasted mug of tea with two sugars and a slice of sponge cake.

Steven grinned. "Well that was a brief visit, hope the old dear doesn't get blown away."

Later that evening in a bedroom still without curtains they went to bed both with a feeling of unfinished business. There was a mass of unpacking to be done and even with the bed made and the central heating going full belt it felt like they were camping out. They lay in each other's arms glad to have the loving contact that made all else appear trivial.

"I wonder what James would have thought of the cottage." As soon as Sam had uttered the words she added "Sorry Steven I shouldn't have said that, just being morbid I suppose."

"No matter my darling love, but please remember this. I loved the boy as well even though I wasn't his real dad."

"I know you did, I'm sorry."

Tired out after their busy and emotional day they did eventually get some much needed sleep.

There followed several days of putting up curtains, unpacking boxes, going to sales to pick up odd bits of furniture and finally getting back to work. March came and went, the days got longer, signs of growth appeared in their new rather overgrown garden.

As the months passed Sam's belly began to show the signs of a baby being in there. She was lucky in that apart from a few early days of morning sickness she had felt no adverse affects of being pregnant. Now as she grew she was proud of the swelling that indicated only too clearly her condition.

There were things to consider such as maternity leave, how and when that was to be taken, preparing the nursery, buying all the stuff that all parents need for a new arrival. She was quite clear in her own mind that the arrival of a baby, no matter how much she was going to love it, was not going to prevent her carrying out her social services role. After all she's done this before so knew the ropes. She would love her child but not to the exclusion of all else. Stephen went along with her thoughts on all this although if the truth were known he would have been happier if his enthusiastic wife had decided at least for the first year of the baby's life to stop work and just be a mum.

Anyway whatever Stephen thought Sam was already making enquiries about baby-minders in the area of their new home. As it happened it was then that Agnes Dalgetty, the woman with the cake all those weeks ago, reappeared on the scene to offer her services. Sam's immediate reaction, when the woman mentioned she was an experienced childminder, was to shy away from the

139

offer. After all Agnes did give the impression of being a bit scatterbrained and the last thing Sam wanted was for the person looking after her child to leave it behind in a shop or something like that. When the woman indignantly produced evidence of her experience in the bab- minding field, Sam began to have second thoughts. In fact it would be very convenient indeed to have baby-minder just two doors away from where they lived. After some persuasion Stephen agreed to accept Agnes in the role of looking after their baby when it arrived. That was after a decent interval from the date of the birth.

Sam didn't take advantage of her full entitlement to maternity leave by any means, bearing the child inside her with healthy acceptance of what was happening to her body. After all she had James while she was studying hard at university and managed quite well. Of course Stephen worried about what he called her devil-may-care attitude towards the process, but then his wife appeared so happy in herself that it was difficult to worry very much so he gradually adopted a similar stance.

All that relaxation vanished when in the early hours of a June morning the discomforting pain Sam had suffered over the last few days became something far more serious.

"This really is it Steve. Get dressed and get the car ready." She clenched her body as the next spasm hit her like a lightning bolt. Within ten minutes they were on their way to Royal Kent hospital in Canterbury.

Sam remained cheerful during her relatively short period of labour, all the while clinging on to Stephen's hand and digging him with her finger nails until he grunted with the pain. The baby girl weighed 7.5 pounds. She was healthy little thing the midwife said with lungs on her like a deep sea diver. Sam was tired but happy, lying back in the bed with her eyes closed, glad that it was all over.

"Nothing to this child bearing thing," she joked all the while smiling dreamily at her husband. Stephen himself was in tears when they brought back his spruced up daughter to put her in his arms.

If the truth were known Sam did suffer of few moments when the old grief about losing James flooded back into her mind. How he would have loved a little sister to protect and dote on, she thought. But then being the lovely child she remembered, he would want her to love this new rival for his mother's affections. Later after the baby's first feed, and with Sam fast asleep in the bed Stephen did some thinking himself. He had wanted to be a dad and now he was. It was almost certainly the happiest day of his life. He couldn't wait to pass on the news to both his and Sam's families.

They kept Sam in overnight leaving Stephen to ring round the relations to tell them the good news. His mother, Miranda, and Maggie and Trylon were of course delighted at the news of their grandchild's birth and promised to pass on the news to other member of their families.

The next day Stephen picked up Sam and the baby and brought them back to Matchstick Cottage. They hadn't been back more than half an hour when the door bell rang to reveal Agnes Dalgetty on their door step with a wide beam of her face and a bunch of flowers in her arms. They could hardly not invite the old dear in and introduce her to the new arrival who was fast asleep in her carrycot.

"What are you going to call this little angel?"

That was indeed a question because, even after long hours of discussion, they still hadn't decided on a name for their baby daughter. Agnes was so excited that she spilt half the mug of tea Stephen had given her on the floor.

Stephen's eyes met Sam's across the room maybe thinking 'and this is the woman in whose care we're going to leave our precious daughter' yet Sam only smiled back. Nothing was going to make her feel other than overjoyed on this lovely bright day, literally as well as in her heart.

When finally they managed to get rid of Agnes and Sam had fed the baby they sat together on the sofa to tackle the important question of naming their offspring. That took time and several glasses of wine before they arrived at a short list of Virginia, Aurelia, Letitia and Blaise, settling in the end on Blaise. By that time Blaise was crying indicating the start of many long sleepless nights to come.

Then came the visits. Sam knew that her mum and dad had been devastated when James died. This new birth she hoped would lessen their mourning for their lost grandson. They couldn't wait to see their little grandaughter so came to visit even though Matchstick Cottage wasn't yet fully furnished. Sam and Stephen had to rush out and buy a double bed so at least Maggie and Trylon had something to sleep on. The truth was that Sam's parents were so over the moon they wouldn't have cared if they'd had to sleep on the floor. It was a happy weekend with Maggie going over the top shopping in Canterbury for a pile of baby things and toys she thought Blaise might appreciate as she got old enough to appreciate them.

Then naturally Miranda Bradbury wanted to see her grandchild so that was another weekend taken up with joy and expenditure. After two weekends running with visits from grandparents Stephen and Sam were glad to have some time to themselves They both understood only too well the happiness the birth of their child had brought to their parents but now they wanted a weekend when they could get to know Blaise on their own and begin to understand the loving responsibility they'd taken on.

Sam loved her baby daughter but the she also loved her job. After four and a half months of dedicated baby care she decided it was time to hand over the care to Agnes. Carl was glad to see her back. As everyone in the service knew 25% of vacancies in social services throughout the country remained unfilled. It was not quite that bad in Kent. Nevertheless he was very glad to have a respected and experienced worker back in the fold.

All through Sam's first day back at work she agonised over the child she had left in the care of a stranger. She needn't have worried, returning home to find Blaise lying peacefully in her carrycot with a delighted Agnes standing guard, well sitting actually, with a beaming smile on her face, although there were a few strands of straggly hair escaping from her normally tight bun which spoke of some slight stress.

"Little dear, good as gold," Agnes cooed her report.

Sam looked down at the small face of her daughter and into those limpid solemn eyes which seemed to say 'where the hell have you been all day, leaving me in the hands of that scatty old biddy.'

Agnes appeared reluctant to let Sam take Blaise away, adjusting her blanket in the baby's cot and generally fussing about the hand-over. There was even a tear in the old woman's eye as Sam carried her daughter away to her real home. Nevertheless the first day of leaving her baby with someone else to look after it had gone off well, and Blaise had accepted it without a qualm as far as Sam could see.

Being reunited with her baby daughter banished all that day-long anxiety. Now she watched with delight as she leant over the carry-cot her face close to the baby's to see her open her eyes, yawn broadly and smile up at her mother. It was one of her very first smiles and Sam wished Stephen had been here to see it. This parenting business was not as difficult as some made out. The love lavished on her child by dear old Agnes appeared almost as good as her own or was she just justifying her decision to go back to work so early after Blaise was born.

Later that same night woken by the baby's plaintiff cries she might have been thinking rather differently hadn't Stephen hauled himself wearily from beneath the duvet to go downstairs to prepare the bottle, then back up to silence his greedy little girl. Some time later Sam was sleepily aware of Stephen's return to their bed having laid down their child in the cot which was part of the largesse bestowed on them by Maggie and Trylon during their visit. She welcomed him lovingly into her arms, quietly enjoyed indulging her husband's sleepy desires before they both fell into a deep post- coital sleep. The last thing Sam heard before she drifted away was a soft murmur from beside her. "I love you."

Chapter 20

They hadn't planned it, hadn't even discussed it. They were happy with their lovely daughter Blaise, now in nursery school and enjoying every minute of it, always full of undecipherable chatter when either Sam or Steven picked her up. But there it was, the pills weren't infallible after all and Sam was most definitely pregnant again. That evening back in Matchstick Cottage, with her little girl tucked up in bed and fast asleep, Sam suggested Steven pour himself a stiff whisky.

"Do I need one sweetheart?"

"You might just at that." She was smiling yet Steven recognised a touch of anxiety in that smile. "I had this feeling a couple of days ago, tested it out this morning. According to Boots I'm going to be a mother again, should be getting good at it with all this practice."

Steven didn't move for what seemed like an age although in truth was a few seconds. Then he very carefully replaced the decanter on the sideboard before turning to look at Sam with a look of delight on his face

"Come here you lovely woman."

For the nest five minutes or so they remained clinging together, tears running down Sam's cheeks and Steven all choked up too.

"What do you think then husband? We haven't really talked about having another baby have we?"

Steven held Sam at arm's length, grinning all over his face before bringing her to him again to kiss her avidly. "You clever little girl."

"Well that's the easy bit. Now we've got a lot of thinking to do financially and otherwise."

Steven blew out his breath in a great gust, shaking his head in apparent disbelief. "To hell with all that practical stuff let's just enjoy the miracle of another brother or sister for Blaise for now." He couldn't keep still, striding about the room, stopping every so often to kiss Sam before ending up at the sideboard again to pour them both a large whisky and Canada dry. "You won't be able to do this from now on," he joked as he took a couple of large swigs of the amber liquid.

"Shall we tell Blaise, do you think?"

"No she wouldn't understand yet, perhaps when I begin to show we can explain then that there's a baby in there."

"I know one person who'll be more than delighted when we eventually tell her and that's Agnes Dalgetty. She was devastated when we decided to send Blaise to nursery school."

"Better make an appointment with lovely Doc Morris in the morning, not that I'm in any doubt but I should get myself checked over, don't you think lover?"

"Of course sweetheart but let's wait a little while before telling the family, shall we? Let's keep our precious secret to ourselves until we get used to the idea."

"You all right with this Steven?" Sam had thought what he had just said displayed a touch of doubt or perhaps worry.

"Yes of course although I do need some time to get my head round being a dad again that's all."

"Nice bit of steak for dinner. Are you still hungry after the shock?" Sam was half joking, half thinking that changing the subject for the time being wouldn't be a bad idea. Steven's reaction after his first burst of delight was rather different than she'd expected. All became clear after dinner when after doing the washing up in the kitchen Steven stopped drying.

"Sam," he said and then nothing.

"Yes Steven what is it?"

"Well don't get me wrong I'm delighted we're going to have another child but...."

"But what Steven?"

"Maybe I think we should have discussed it first, you know what I mean."

Sam laughed but there wasn't much humour there. "I see, you think I stopped taking the pill without consulting you?"

"Well didn't you?"

"No I didn't." She gave him a hard look. Bloody hell how could the man think such a thing. "In fact it just goes to show that the good old pill isn't infallible doesn't it?"

"Oh."

"Yes, 'oh', you don't have much faith in me do you Steven if you thought what you implied."

Steven grimaced, feeling all the disgrace of someone found out in an embarrassing situation. "Sorry Sam, I'm just a damn fool, please forgive me for doubting you."

The truth was that Sam partly blamed herself. She should have made it clear from the start that she hadn't stopped taking the pill. Had she done that on purpose, some sort of test of her husband, she wondered and wouldn't have been able to give an answer.

It wasn't a serious rift they both said to themselves but when Steven tried to draw Sam into his arms in bed that night she pulled gently away. "Sorry Steven I'm whacked out, just want to get some sleep." She heard his sigh and instantly regretted her action but it was done. She'd make it up to him tomorrow.

In the morning it was all go, getting Blaise up, dressed fed and ready to go to nursery school. Yet amongst the early morning hustle and bustle both of them tripped over themselves each trying to say sorry to the other for last night's slight tiff about birth control. There wasn't time for much else as they both had appointments booked as part of their busy days.

It was a cold December day with the wind blowing from the north and the threat of snow in the air. The thought crossed Sam's mind, as she settled her daughter into her car seat how delighted and amazed the little girl would be if it actually did snow. She'd never seen snow; that was a treat to come maybe.

"What snow mummy?"

An amused Sam smiled back at the child sitting wrapped up in the seat behind her. "You remember sweetheart, that story about a snowman we watched on television, that was snow."

"Like that," Blaise produced a little chuckle of laughter at the memory of the film.

It was later that same day, when after a particularly harrowing case conference which had resulted in a decision to apply to the local authority for an interim care order, that Sam met up with Rosie Temple, another care worker on a similar grade to her.

"You look done in Sam."

"Child neglect case, interim care order and from what I can see the parents are just stupid enough not to heed the warning. I can see two little boys being taken into care before many weeks are out and I always hate that."

"We all do, love, but the protection of the child must get priority you must agree."

"Of course I do but some parents have such miserable lives themselves it's hard not to feel sorry for them and understand their less than caring dealings with their kids."

Then with a sudden change of subject Rosie sighed and asked, "Everything alright between you and Steven is it?"

Sam's eyebrows shot up in surprise. "Everything's fine." She was tempted to mention her pregnancy but it was much too early so she continued, "Why on earth should you ask that?"

Rosie looked slightly disconcerted. "Oh nothing I just thought......."

"For Christ's sake Rosie, you just thought what?"

"Nothing Sam, really, I was just interested in how the two of you were getting along that's all."

Sam had made an appointment with Doctor Morris first thing that morning to see him early afternoon so her conversation with Rosie petered out, but it left her with a sense of uneasy curiosity. There was something there that she couldn't quite put her finger on and she didn't like the feeling. On the other hand the visit to the surgery went off happily with the doctor confirming that she was about six weeks pregnant and in robust good health. Doctor Morris was quite young, very much in touch with his patients' backgrounds, seeming to really care about them.

"Lovely for Blaise to have a little brother or sister don't you agree Sam. I always think an only child is rather a sad thing although I shouldn't say things like that." He offered Sam his usual avuncular smile, holding on to her hand a little longer than was normal as they said goodbye. He obviously loved this part of his job, his pleasure apparent in his beaming smile.

Later that day, back in Matchstick Cottage with Blaise full of fish-fingers and lying on her tummy watching a cartoon on CBBC, Sam waited for Steven to get home, eager to tell him a about her visit to Doc Morris that morning.

He was late. In fact he'd been getting back late quite a lot lately not that she read anything into that. In their jobs nothing was nine to five, there were always minor crises that had to be dealt with, but they'd made a sort of pact that Friday nights would be special, a precursor to the weekend when they could make plans so when he was late that night she was disappointed.

Putting that to one side Sam got on with preparing their evening meal even stopping to sit down on the floor next to Blais, soaking in some of the delight the child was experiencing watching the magic screen in front of her. God what a boon television was to families with young children she thought as she smiled at the antics displayed in front of her. The programme ended just then, and the little girl turned her slightly frowning face towards her mother.

"No snow."

"No darling not yet but perhaps it will snow for Christmas."

"Promise."

"Well I can't do that sweetheart. We'll just have to wait and see, won't we?"

At that moment they heard the front door opening. The child bounded to her feet, rushed out of the door and flung herself into Steven's arm with cries of "Daddy, Daddy."

Sam thought he looked rather tired as he hugged the child close to his chest. "Steady on young lady. One of these days you're going to do that and I'll drop you on your head." He smiled but again his expression appeared to Sam to be rather dour, not the usual brightness with which he usually greeted his little daughter.

Then at the point when Sam thought she was due a hug too, Steven lowered the child to the floor, walked across to the sideboard where the drinks were kept and asked wearily if his wife would like a gin and tonic.

"Lovely. Had a bad day Steven?"

That night Sam had her recurring nightmare. It always happened if she was unsettled or worried about something. In the nightmare the scene was always different but the crux of the situation was always the same in that she was lost and desperate to find her way to some particular place. That night she'd been on a railway station waiting for a train and, with time to spare, she'd wandered out of the station to take a short stroll along the street just passing time. Then, when she turned to go back to the station, she couldn't find the right road. Increasingly desperate she tried one route after another but none was familiar. She was going to miss her train, she had to find that damn station, she was terribly anxious, desperately worried but above all frustrated at her inability to find her way back to the station. In those dreams she never knew what happened in the end but they always left her with a residue of anxiety for some time after she woke.

In the morning she woke feeling frazzled as she always did after one of her nightmares. But life goes on, little girls want their breakfast and want those around them to take notice of their babbling efforts to communicate. Steven was never at his brightest first thing in the morning and that morning he was even grumpier than usual. Sam's request that he take Blaise into nursery was rebuffed by an almost angry assertion that he had a very full and early programme in the office. Of course Sam didn't really mind, she loved the child's chatter as they drove into town yet she had thought the little girl's father might like that enjoyment himself once in a while. From her child seat in the back of the car Blaise was still chattering about snow, apparently complaining about why it hadn't arrived yet.

Christmas that year was an exciting experience for Blaise. The previous year she had enjoyed the experience without fully realising what was going on. Now at two and a half years old she relished the whole magical experience right from the time when the shops began to display Christmas fare. She enjoyed the host of seasonal films on TV and the toy adverts as well. They invited Trylon and Maggie down for a few days over the festive period so the little girl was spoiled something rotten. Steven seemed to have got over his grumpy spell and joined in the celebrations with the rest of the family. They hadn't told anyone yet about Sam's pregnancy.

Blaise had her own little bed now not that she stayed in it long on Christmas morning. Despite having a large stocking which was supposed to keep her occupied for a while at least, she came running into her parents' bedroom to jump unceremonious on their bed. Then after squeals of excitement went to make sure her grandparents weren't missing out on the fun. Presents were supposed to be opened after breakfast in an organised way but that didn't happen. Blaise eventually disappeared under a pile of wrapping paper undecided which toy she wanted to play with first. Finally persuaded to have some breakfast still in her slippers and dressing gown, she was the first to notice that outside the windows there was a faint fluttering of snow.

She pushed her little nose right up against the window pain and shouted, "Snow, snow, snow." The adults came to look and sure enough large snowflakes were drifting down in the crisp morning air and in one or two spots small piles of snow were accumulating. Sam good-humourdly got the child dressed in warm clothing, almost as excited as Blaise by snow on Christmas Day, before letting her out into the garden where she scooped up handfuls from the sparse deposits, throwing it up in the air in joyful abandon. Trylon followed her out and watched as she played with the snow enjoying the child's delight with this new thing in her life.

Maggie was a dab hand in the kitchen and virtually took control of the Christmas dinner preparations with Sam in amused and possibly relieved attendance. Steven after venturing briefly into the garden to watch his daughter trying to make something out of the meague falls of snow, appeared subdued to the point where even Maggie noticed and said quietly to Sam in the kitchen.

"Everything alright between you two Sam?"

Sam smiled, she was happy that Christmas morning surrounded as she was by people she loved most in the world. "Yes of course, why do you ask?"

"He seems very quiet that's all love."

"He's fine mum, probably just tired. He was working right up to Christmas Eve."

The dinner went down well, the turkey roasted to perfection, Blaise with more than her share of assisted cracker pulling. As they all sat back replete from the feast Steven's mobile rang. He hurried out of the room to take the call. When he came back he had on his doleful face.

"Sorry Sam, and everyone, that was my mum. It appears Michael couldn't get over from Brussels after all and so she's all on her own. She just wanted to make contact and wish us all a happy Christmas but I feel I should drive over to visit her for a few hours. Shouldn't take me too long to get to Bromley today, not much traffic I hope.

Sam immediately began to think of ways round the situation. "Why didn't you invite her over here Steven?"

"I did love, but she didn't fancy the drive. Look I'm sorry folks but I do feel I should go over."

Of course they all went along with Steven's decision to go and see his lonely mum yet somewhere at the back of Sam's mind there lurked faint suspicion and she hated herself for it. Steven wouldn't betray her would he? She forced the idea out of her mind chiding herself for thinking it in the first place. Yet with Steven away she was subdued for the rest of the day not that, as far as she knew, anybody noticed. Luckily Blaise took centre stage for most of the day until eventually she fell asleep tired out after all the excitement.

Every Christmas since she'd left Sheffield Sam had exchanged Christmas cards with her old friend Jason Anderson and occasionally they'd had a 'how are you getting on' exchange of emails. Now for some reason as Sam meditated on her vague suspicions about her husband, Jason came into her mind. She remembered him fondly, not the most dynamic of men yet a gentle soul for all that. She wondered what had happened to him, had he married, did he have a partner. These things had never been mentioned in the sparse email communication they'd had over the years. She found herself watching the television without taking in what she was watching. When Maggie asked her if she wanted a cup of tea she had to jerk herself back to the here and now.

"Yes thanks mum. I was miles away."

"Thinking about poor Steven I suppose."

It got late and Sam somehow knew there would be no sign of Steven that night. When eventually he rang to say he thought he better stay over she wasn't at all surprised, saying nothing to persuade him otherwise. She went to bed full of thoughts she might very well regret in the morning and chiding herself for her suspicious nature. As she lay there tossing and turning the thing that got to her most was why she should have all those suspicions in the first place. After all Steven was a good husband and a loving father. Why on earth should she suspect him of being anything else? Yet the niggle wouldn't go away. It was as though some vague instinct was telling her to be wary. And then there was Maggie and her comment earlier in the evening about Steven being quiet. Perhaps she had sensed something too.

Before she finally dropped off to sleep she came to the conclusion that she would ring Miriam in the morning to enquire casually if Steven was on his way back. She would have to word it all very carefully so that her mother-in-law wouldn't realise she was investigating the whereabouts of her son but that at least it would dispel doubt and doubt dispelled was what she needed in her present state of mind.

Nor surprisingly she slept fitfully that night and awoke with a sense of apprehension at what she had promised herself she would do that morning. She fed Blaise her breakfast and then disappeared into the bedroom to make the call.

"Hello Sam, great to hear from you. How's Blaise?"

"She's having a lovely time spoiled rotten by my mum and dad of course. What about you, what kind of Christmas have you had?"

Miranda failed to fully disguise her sigh. " Well I had Christmas dinner with my next-door neighbours. As you probably heard Michael couldn't make it home in time but there you are that's families for you." There had been no mention of her other son.

Sam had heard all she wanted or rather didn't want to hear. She made polite conversation for a short while which including asking her mother-in-law to come over and see Blaise, but her brain was dead. Steven was playing away and at Christmas time as well. What was she going to do now? Come right out with it and face her husband with her suspicions. Wait and see what happened when Steven came home as she expected him to do some time today? Mention that she'd been on the phone to Mrs. Bradbury and wait for the reaction. It was all shit. Whatever she did there was now no doubt in her mind that her bastard husband had been unfaithful.

Curiously it was worry about what she would say to Steven if and when he did come home that bothered her most. Here she was with a two and a half year old daughter and another new life in her belly. She had a lot to lose and did it really matter if her husband was screwing another woman. Of course it did. Betrayal, that's what it would be, betrayal of all the trust she had invested in their intimacy, in a relationship she thought was loving and sound. "Hello Steven how was your girlfriend?" Something like that. Or "You fucking cheating bastard get the hell out of my sight." Maggie and Trylon were still there of course. She didn't want to send them home worrying about their daughter. It was her problem. At the end of all her distracted thinking the conclusion was that she would say nothing, at least for the time being. Cowardly mayb,e but she couldn't bring herself to cast the first brick no matter how justified it was.

Steven did come back to Matchstick cottage just in time for lunch, gave all the right answers to the questions asked about his mother's welfare, drank rather more glasses of wine than usual, but otherwise Sam could detect nothing different about him. Her inner thoughts were still in turmoil yet she managed to get through the day thanks to the presence of her parents and the constant needs of her little girl. Come bed time however she found it difficult to maintain her feelings. There were no warming up cuddles that night. It was as though there was an unspoken truce between them that for the time being they would exist side by side as usual but only exist, nothing else. The days to come would not be tranquil but for the time being or at least for that night nothing was said to break the truce.

Chapter 21

There was that delicious early morning coolness in the air as Sam ventured out into the garden at the rear of her beloved cottage. There were still some daffodils left although most of them were now past their best. As she stood there breathing in the smell of spring, she was joined by a lively little girl eager for one more day of adventure. Then they were three as Jason Anderson came up behind them and placed an arm round both their shoulders in affectionate greeting.

Jason's visit had lifted Sam's spirits. She wasn't looking for any serious renewed relationship. She'd had enough of those for the time being, but his gentle presence around the cottage cheered her up no end. It also gave her a faintly malicious pleasure to see Steven's reaction to her visitor's presence when he called to take Blaise out for the day. He'd buggered off to his new woman, yet he still appeared to resent what might have been construed as the new man in her life, not that he was in fact, but she enjoyed the hanging possibility as far as her ex-husband was concerned.

"Is Jason going to live with us Mummy?"

Jason grinned, Sam smiled. "That would be lovely darling, but no he's just here on a visit. Actually he's an old friend from when I was living in Sheffield."

The little girl suddenly turned shy and whispered to her mother, "I like Jason mummy."

The two young people liked each other but boy were there barriers to anything more. Here was Sam wounded from her recent divorce, mother of one little girl and pregnant with another child. Here was Jason wary of responsibility, of a loving nature yet a scatterbrained personality. There was never going to be anything more than a tender friendship between those two, was there?

And so it came about. As always intended, Jason packed his bag on Sunday afternoon, loaded it into his ancient Saab and with tears in his eyes kissed Sam goodbye and Blaise too. When he drove away Sam felt bereft. Her little girl knew only too well that something sad had happened between their visitor and her mum. She cuddled up in Sam's arms, sensing her mother's pain without really understanding why she was hurting so badly.

Sadness was interrupted by the bustling arrival of Agnes Dalgetty through the garden gate. "Your visitor gone then love?. Thought you might like a bunch of these tulips."

In the circumstances Sam could hardly not invite the old dear in for a cup of tea although in truth she would far rather have done some quiet ruminating on her own. She found her attention slipping as Agnes chatted away but luckily the old lady was quite involved listening to the little girl's tales about what they'd done while Jason had been with them. She was brought back to the moment by hearing Blaise say, "I really liked Jason Auntie Agnes."

That didn't help her mood one little bit and she was glad when Agnes decided she had chores to do at home, making her profuse goodbyes before rushing off as quickly as she'd arrived.

Monday morning was much like any other Monday morning, nothing surprising when Cart Rocklove invited her into his office, although she was surprised when her rather nervous boss asked her sit down as he had something to say to her.

"Sam, I usually advocate not mixing social and work lives but we've known each other for a while now and I ......," He stopped, shuffled some papers round on his desk, looked down and then up, "well I wondered if you would like me take you out to dinner one evening?"

Sam realised at that moment that she didn't really know much about Carl's personal life although somewhere at the back of her mind she remembered someone saying that he'd been divorced for some time. To say she was surprised was putting it mildly. She's always thought of Carl as just a genial boss but never as someone who might have an interest in her as a woman.

"Well I........," she started to say.

"Look Sam no big deal. If I've embarrassed you forget it. I just thought it would be nice to get out of the office and have a chat about things in general."

She'd never seen him look so self conscious in all the time she'd known him. Now she had to say something to answer the question that hung in the air waiting for her next move.

"That would be lovely Carl. Are you saying that it would involve some sort of assessment?"

Carl laughed. "Not very good at this sort of thing am I? No Sam my invitation is personal. I would enjoy having dinner with you because I like you, nothing to do with work I can assure you."

They settled on the coming Friday. Sam would have to get confirmation, but she didn't think there would be any problem in getting Agnes Dalgetty to babysit for the evening. She left the office in something of a haze. It has all been so unexpected, yet as she walked away down the corridor towards the general office where she had her desk, she felt as frisson of excitement and unexpected pleasure surge through her body. It was a while since a man had taken her out to dinner. She had to admit the proposition was exciting. Since her breakup with Steven she hadn't even thought about such possibilities concentrating on work and her daughter almost to the exclusion of everything else.

When Carl called to pick her up at Matchstick Cottage on Friday evening she felt as nervous as a young girl out on her first date. She had known Carl for several years as a boss, but now she had to think of him in a different light and that took some doing. She knew very little about the man although office gossip had provided the detail that he was divorced so there was nothing illicit about this outing. She knew him as a kind and considerate boss and when she came to think of it he wasn't bad looking. Tonight would, she hoped, fill out the outline picture she had of the man.

Carl had booked a table at the Oscar and Bentley's bistro in Canterbury. On the drive into the city their conversation was bland, not touching on anything very personal. Carl was solicitous but nervous and that had the effect of making Sam nervous too. They had a quick drink at the bar before sitting down at their table, Carl with alcohol free beer and Sam with whisky and Canada dry.

"Do you have children Carl?"

Children were perhaps a safe subject. Carl knew about Blaise of course, and her pregnancy as well which had made it all the more strange that he should have invited her out to dinner, she thought.

"No, sadly, my ex-wife didn't like the idea of us having kids, that may have been one of the reasons for our breakup."

Sam, seeing the pain in his eyes, decided not to pursue that avenue any further. Realising the sensitivity of her question brought Sam round to thinking about her own situation. Having dinner with a work colleague was one thing. Did she want it to be another thing? Carl was obviously aware that she was, to put it crudely, available as a runner in the mating stakes. Two divorced adults getting together, nothing wrong with that was there? But what did she want? Was she looking for another relationship, and if she was why hadn't she responded to her recent visitor's obvious interest. She was fond of gentle Jason yet wasn't prepared to commit herself to anything permanent. After all they had given it a try all those years ago. It hadn't worked then although of course the circumstances were very different.

"How's little Blaise, three now isn't she?"

That was safe ground. For a few minutes she recited tales of Blaise's adventures to their mutual amusement. The waiter came up just then to interrupt her flow and they ordered their food in the hiatus that followed. Carl appeared to be making heavy weather of their evening with breaks in the conversation when he appeared at a loss of what to say. May be he was just out of practice at the dating game.

The food was good and formed a conversational conduit that kept things moving for a while but then, after saying no shop talk, Carl moved onto cases he had overseen recently. The awkward diner became an enthusiastic advocate of his daytime job, a different personality altogether. Sam had always liked Carl ever since she'd joined the service, but liked him as a considerate boss. Now in this social environment it didn't seem right somehow.

The pair relaxed on the drive home, probably both relieved that the awkward encounter would soon be coming to an end.

The "You're back early." from Agnes Dalgetty didn't help.

Sam smiled. "We've both got a full diary for tomorrow Agnes. Anyway we had a lovely meal didn't we Carl?"

Of course he enthusiastically agreed, yet declined the offer of coffee, said he'd better be getting back although both of them knew there was no need to rush off.

The two women listened to the car drive away in the night. Agnes directed a quizzical look on her young friend. "Not what you'd hoped love?"

Sam shook her head slightly. "He's a lovely man Agnes, no really, but for some reason neither of us felt relaxed, and I can't tell you why.

Agnes gathered her things together before leaving for her short walk home. Sam, left on her own, felt disorientated somehow. She liked Carl, she thought Carl liked her, so why had the evening been such a disaster? She poured herself a generous tot of whisky with a hint of dry ginger, tried to watch the news, but couldn't concentrate, thinking instead of how she and Carl would react when they met each other the next day. On the way upstairs, having decided to make an early night of it, she peeped in at the sleeping Blaise to enjoy the sight of her beautiful little daughter.sleeping so peacefully.

Chapter 22

I'm sure it's only a viral infection so I'm not going to prescribe antibiotics Sam. The middle ear can become a bit infected which is where the discomfort comes from. However I'm sure the child's immune system will resolve the problem fairly quickly. Blaise wasn't usually a winey child, but when she'ds woken up several times during the night Sam was worried that the earache she was complaining about might be something serious which is why they were there that morning in the doctor's surgery.

Sam and Simon Morris had been using their Christian namesfor several years now. Over the years Sam had built an absolute trust in the man. He was marvellous with children, had a knack of putting them at their ease whatever the problem. Today, if he said there was nothing to worry about, then there was nothing to worry about.

"You had all your scans then Sam?" The doctor glanced meaningfully in the direction of her stomach.

She smiled. It was easy to smile at Simon. He just made you want to respond to his own smiles. "Yes thanks Simon. I'm going to have a little boy."

Sam was very fond of Doctor Simon Morris, although when she thought about it she knew very little about Simon Morris the man, didn't even know if he was married or had any kids of his own. Must have would have been her guess, charming guy like that, natural dad.

"I was sorry to hear that you and Steven had split up Sam, and at a time when a husband would have come in pretty useful." For once he wasn't smiling, his concern for her welfare was apparent. She could feel it coming through to her senses as a wave of sympathy.

Doctors are very busy these days so Sam left him to it. On the way back home Blaise was already showing signs of perking up, the magic Doc Morrison touch had worked again so it seemed. Sam didn't want to take any more time off than necessary so she left the little girl in the care of Agnes Dalgetty and drove into work to pick up a couple of cases that had been earmarked for her attention. The rest of the day passed off without serious problems and when she picked Blaise up in the evening the little girl was full of beans and virtually back to her normal lively little self. Agnes had already given her tea so Sam sat her down in front of the television to watch CBBCs before taking her upstairs to bed.

It was some time later with Blaise bathed and fast asleep in bed that the front doorbell rang. To Sam's surprise there on the doorstep stood that same Simon Morrison she'd seen that morning although now looking a little sheepish.

"How's your little girl Sam?"

Sam was taken aback for a few seconds by the unexpectedness of the call. After that moment's hesitation she stood back ushering the doctor inside. "Good gracious Simon I didn't know the NHS ran to home visits these days."

Simon laughed. "No we don't but I've been to collect a couple of books from a shop in Canterbury so I thought I'd call in on the way past."

165

That didn't ring true but on the other hand why else should a doctor be calling. They stood there in the hallway until finally Sam got round to inviting her visitor into the living room, asking him to sit down and offering him a cup of tea.

"Blaise is fast asleep now Simon." Sam had returned with the promised cup of tea which she handed over with questions running through her brain like an old-fashioned pocket calculator.

"Yes of course but you can still tell me how she is can't you, Sam?"

Sam sat down opposite the doctor, still uncertain about the situation she now found herself in. "She's much better thanks Simon. I'm expecting her to be back to her usual bundle of energy by tomorrow. You didn't really call to enquire about the health of my daughter did you Simon?"

"I'm always interested in the health of my patients, you know that Sam." He seemed nervous, kept picking up and putting down the mug of tea Sam had given him and grinning for no particular reason. "But I'll admit I did have another motive for calling. Over the years you've told me so much about this cottage of yours, Matchstick Cottage I believe it's called, I wanted to see it for myself."

Sam looked at him still with disbelief in her eyes. "You mean you went out of your way just to see a country cottage."

Simon Morrison was looking sheepish again. He took a deep breath. "Alright I wanted to see you Sam, probably a breach of medical ethics but there it is, guilty as charged. I was hoping I might invite you out to dinner some time and it seemed more appropriate to do it away from the surgery. I've been wanting to make a move in that direction for some time and by the way I really did pick up a book in Canterbury."

"You must be joking Simon. Why on earth would you want to date a very pregnant woman with a three year old daughter in tow? To say Sam was gob-smacked was putting it mildly. True she had always had a soft spot for the amenable doctor but she'd never thought of him in the way that was now being indicated. She knew nothing of his background. She assumed he didn't have a partner in view of his invitation but had no idea if he was divorced anything like that.

"Taken you by surprise have I Sam?"

"You can say that again. I need a drink, a stiff one. How about you?"

"I'm sorry Sam. I've gone about this in a totally wrong way but," he stopped to smile, "I can assure you that my intentions are entirely honourable."

Sam sat there sipping the gin she ought not to be drinking, shaking her head slowly from side to side still with a shocked look on her face. Yet part of her brain was messaging "Why not?" in certain circumstances. After all there would be no shocks for Simon, he already knew about her family in some detail. She liked the man and although he was perhaps ten years older than her the age gap wasn't significant at their time of life.

"Look Simon I do like you but I've never thought of you in a social context. This has all come as a bit of a shock, you must see that."

Simon blew out his cheeks, producing a meaningful sigh as he lurched to his feet. "OK, Sam, forget my clumsy efforts to invite you out. I'll go now and you can write me off as a medical idiot."

"I'm flattered Simon, really I am. Give me some time to think about it. You're a nice man, certainly not an idiot, medical or otherwise. And I promise I will give your invitation some serious thought."

As Sam heard the sound of Doctor Morris's car driving away she couldn't resist chuckling to herself. Here she was very pregnant, yet Carl, and now Simon had tried to get something going between them. Perhaps pregnant women had a particular attraction for men of which she wasn't aware. That night in her bed while she tried to get her bulky stomach into a position that would allow her to sleep she thought some more about Simon Morrison's invitation. He was an attractive man, she certainly liked him, found him good company so what was wrong with a dinner date? In the end she decided she would invite him over to Matchstick Cottage and give him the chance to sample a bit of home cooking.

So the following Sunday, after Sam had had a serious chat on the telephone to that same Doctor Simon Morrison, it was arranged that he would come round to Matchstick Cottage for lunch. The serious bit of the conversation had been about her telling her prospective guest-to-be not to read anything more into the invitation than was intended, and that was a friendly get-together between two people who liked each other. Of course the good doctor accepted the condition without a qualm, arriving at the cottage with flowers for Sam and a bag of grotesque sweets for Blaise, after which he was her friend for life.

It was a warm day and they had their seafood salad outside on the lawn at the back of the cottage. "You've got a lovely spot here Sam. And this garden, you must have green fingers."

"That bit outside the back door is mine uncle Simon."

He was already a hit with the child after the sweets and taking an interest in some of her recent art work from play school. At once he let himself be led by the hand to see the flowers the little girl had grown. Sam watched the couple enjoying the obvious rapport between the two of them. He would certainly make a great dad she thought before quickly banishing such thought from her mind. She wasn't looking for any relationships right now, although with another mood swing, it did occur to her that in her position of shortly becoming the mother of two very young children a man might just come in useful.

It was a very pleasant afternoon, extending into the evening when Simon read a bedtime story to an excited little girl. Once again thoughts flickered through Sam's mind about how nice it was for children to have someone of both sexes in their domestic life. When her visitor had driven away Sam had to admit to herself that she was left with a warm glow. She smiled to herself. What was she thinking about? Did she really see the kind doctor as some sort of partner? Did she even fancy him, which was an important question? It was no good having the ideal man on paper as it were if she didn't fancy the pants off him.

In the days that followed Simon's visit to Matchstick Cottage, he rang her several times to say how much he'd enjoyed his day with Sam and her delightful little daughter and to repeat his invitation for her to have dinner with him. On the third time of asking she accepted. She spent time with her appearance wanting him to find her attractive but at the same time still unsure of her own feelings towards the man. He was easy to like. She'd always liked him ever since her first visit to him as a doctor, but liking was one thing, did she feel anything beyond that? In all honesty she couldn't say and anyway what was wrong with two friends having dinner together.

169

Whether it was fate or not she wouldn't know but her heart gave a little skip when it turned out that Simon had booked the Oscar and Bentleys bistro for their dinner. He was a charming host and Sam thoroughly enjoyed her meal and his company, yet she remained uncertain as to whether she wanted their relationship, if that's what it was, to develop. In fact she wondered if she was being rather o presumptuous in thinking that's what Simon wanted anyway from their short association. Whatever the case it was a relaxed evening. She couldn't help comparing it to the awkwardness of her dinner with Carl, immediately chiding herself for such a churlish thought.

The evening passed quickly and enjoyably. When they arrived back at the cottage it seemed only polite to invite Simon in for a coffee. When she paid Agnes off, and said goodbye, the baby-sitter gave her a smile that appeared to contain a message although quite what Agnes intended by it she didn't know. The two of them continued their easy conversation until at about midnight when Simon, after glancing at his watch, said he should be going. When he kissed her goodbye on the cheek Sam had a half wish he'd kissed her on the mouth but there you are things didn't always work out as you wanted them. She was still left with a glow inside her which spoke of possibilities.

Chapter 23

Sam, in the way of nature, got fatter as she neared her third experience of giving birth. Doctor Simon had been solicitous during those last weeks, had even offered to be her birth partner. She appreciated the attention although she declined the birth partner offer, perhaps there was a degree of intimacy involved for which she wasn't yet ready. Nevertheless it was fair to say that by the time she actually gave birth to her boy baby, they were firm friends. Nothing romantic had occurred between them and this worried Sam. If she was looking for anything at all it wasn't a bosom pal, more a companionable lover.

"Well I see you managed quite well without me." were Simon's first words when he came to visit her to view the new arrival. It had been an easy birth and despite her tiredness Sam was happy to see visitors. Blaise was there, very excited and proud about having a little brother. Agnes had brought her in to visit her mum. She too was over the moon at the thought of having another young child she could cherish and spoil. Carl Rocklove brought her some flowers. Sam introduced the two men and they solemnly shook hands although Sam could see at once that they weren't about to become bosom pals. Maggie and Trylon were quite naturally delighted at the birth of their grandson. They sent flowers and promised an early visit.

Sam went home the next day driven by her doctor friend. She felt happy back in her beloved cottage, happy with the safe arrival of her new son. Although when she looked down on him sleeping peacefully in his crib she suffered a jolt of regret. The child was the very image of James when he was born but then didn't most new-borns look fairly similar. She wiped away a few errant tears, consoling herself that she would never forget James but life had to go on and now little Thomas would have to be the centre of her attention.

Of course Agnes Dalgetty came round to view the new baby she could dote on. Simon stayed for the rest of the day making sure Sam took it easy. Only when, finally, Blaise was in bed and fast asleep and the new baby was away with the fairies too, did Simon take a break.

"Think I deserve a gin and tonic don't you Simon?"

He was up on his feet in a flash to do her bidding while at the same time pouring himself a cold beer from the fridge.

When he came back to the sitting room where a sleepy Sam was waiting for her drink it appeared he had something to say. "Sam, you must have got the message by now that I've become very fond of you and ....." He stopped and sighed, looked rather confused.

"And what Simon? By the way the feeling is reciprocal."

Doctor Morrison ran his hand through his unruly hair. "Well I think I'm just a little bit in love with you Sam, that's what."

Sam smiled. "Only a little bit?" Truth was that she'd enjoyed being spoiled and looked after by this lovely man over the last few weeks yet she still wasn't sure how deep her feelings for him went. She didn't want any misunderstandings between the two of them. It was because of that, that her response had sounded so ambiguous. It was then that he moved closer to her on the sofa to take her in his arms to kiss her properly for the first time. They sat like that for some time without a word, the new mother and the infatuated doctor, happy in the moment but uncertain about tomorrow.

That was the real start if there was a start at all. Actually they continued more or less as they had been doing with Simon spending much of his time at Matchstick cottage although now with sexual overtones. And still Sam didn't know her own mind. Blaise absolutely loved Simon being around. She would have accepted him as her new dad without turning a hair. Steven was to a large extent concentrating on his new partner and perceptive little Blaise sensed his lack of commitment. Although he still took her out every so often he sometimes cut short their outings with some excuse or other.

Sam was happy to let things jog along with Simon staying overnight sometimes, yet going back to his flat over the surgery on other occasions. Blaise had asked her once why Simon didn't just stay at the cottage all the time and she had answered in a non-committal way because she didn't know the answer herself, and it didn't seem to matter in the scheme of things. Neither Sam nor Simon had ever mentioned love yet there was obviously feelings between them that spoke of it. Yet neither of them appeared to want to take that final step to full partnership.

The summer was passing, baby Thomas was growing fast with Blaise in constant caring attention. She loved the whole idea of having a little brother, played with him constantly and, judging by his smiles, he loved all that attention.

Sam went back to work at the beginning of October despite being scolded by Blaise for leaving Thomas with a Agnes Dalgetty. "He's only a little baby mummy, you should look after him yourself. He'll think you don't love him."

No he won't sweetheart. Agnes is very good with babies, don't you remember?"

The little girl frowned, "That was different."

"Why do you say that darling?"

"I don't know it just was." She wasn't to be placated, remaining in a sad mood right up until bedtime. And even when Sam tucked her in and kissed her goodnight, she still appeared to be worried about the fate of her little brother.

When Sam went back downstairs she told Simon about Blaise's reaction to her asking Agnes to look after Thomas and he laughed. "That boy has got a protector for life. I hope he appreciates that when he gets a bit older."

Sam suddenly changed tack, and out of the blue she turned a serious face to look Simon straight in the eye. "I've been meaning to ask you this for a while Simon. Where is this thing between us going would you say?"

Simon ran his hand through his hair, pursed his lips, sighed and then, after a pause shrugged his shoulders. "I thought we were doing alright Sam. I'm very fond of you."

"That doesn't really answer my question does it Simon."

"Perhaps not, but I ask again. What don't you like about where we are now and the way we're living our lives?" That's what he said but the way he said it and the expression on his face showed an obvious uneasiness. It was although he recognised that Sam had a point and he was unsure on how to answer her in a way that sounded anything like logical or even reasonable.

"Look Simon you must know what I mean. Our lifestyle appears transitory. You moving from one place to another. What's more it's unsettling for Blaise. The poor child loves you and doesn't understand why you keep going away every so often."

"You looking for marriage Sam?"

"Not particularly,.but I am looking for some sort of commitment. I don't seem to have been very successful with the men in my life so far and now here I am again in love with a man who isn't sure what he wants out of this particular relationship."

Simon moved across the room to the sideboard to poor himself a whiskey, his face creased in a frown. "You want one Sam?"

She nodded and, with her eyes still asking for an answer, accepted the glass Simon handed her.

"You could both move to the flat." He knew that wasn't what she wanted to hear but he blundered on. "Very convenient for my job and you wouldn't want me to give that up would you?"

"No of course not Simon. Anyway I love Matchstick Cottage and so does Blaise. You're no distance at all from your surgery and you could get to call outs just as easily from here as from your flat."

"You're suggesting I move in with you permanently Sam?"

"What's wrong with that? You're here for half the time anyway."

Simon took a substantial gulp of his whiskey, sighed and blew out his cheeks. "Nothing wrong with that at all except that........."

"Except for what Simon?"

"Well nothing really. Practical things like finance and who pays for what."

Roy Grantham

"If that's all then it's a done deal. Neither of us is particularly mercenary and if two sensible adults can't come to agreement about how to organise their lives it's a bad job, isn't it ?"

She'd won the battle, if battle it was, and now bestowed a loving kiss on the man she wanted to spend the rest of her life with. Simon shook his head slowly from side to side as if recovering from a blow to the chin. But he smiled nonetheless. A defeat perhaps, but a pleasant one.

Chapter 24

Christmas that year was a happy one. Simon had settled in well to life in Matchstick Cottage, finding no problems at all with continuing with his practice duties. Margaret Hampton, his partner, had accepted the situation without demur. In fact she found it rather amusing that her colleague had shacked up with a woman who already had two kids of her own. Each to their own she might have said bearing in mind her own rather turbulent domestic life. Blaise was still intrigued by having a baby brother and young Thomas himself was thriving and taking an interest in all that was going on around him.

Happy but quiet. Trylon had a dose of the flu so Maggie had decided no visit this year, what with a new baby and all. It just wasn't worth the risk. No snow either much to the disappointment of Blaise who still remembered the delight of playing in it last Christmas. Simon was still getting used to family life after living by himself for such a long period but unexpectedly his holiday was disturbed by an urgent call out about half an hour before Sam was about to serve Christmas dinner.

While Simon was away attending to his duties there was hilarity in what remained of the little family when Thomas had his first foray into solids. Blaise loved helping in that exercise and thought the mess on and around the baby's high chair was a source of amusement.

Eventually Simon returned in time to eat his warmed up dinner after his patient had been taken away in an ambulance to hospital and was now in safe hands. It was three o'clock before he pushed his plate away declaring that he couldn't eat another thing. Margaret had taken over the practice call out responsibilities for the rest of the day so Simon could relax and enjoy a couple of glasses of single malt.

Then out of the blue, the happy day was shattered by a telephone call from Maggie. Trylon's flu had taken a serious downturn. The doctor had sent for an ambulance and whisked him off to hospital from where Maggie was now ringing. They hadn't told her specifically what was wrong with her man but suspected it was pneumonia. Of course Sam was worried and asked her mother to keep them in touch with her father's condition. Blaise knew her grandad was ill but hated the gloom that has descended on Matchstick Cottage. It was Christmas Day and she was sorry about her grandad yet didn't quite see why they should stop playing games and having fun.

It came as a slow realisation to Sam of just how serious Trylon's condition could be. People died of pneumonia didn't they? She had always had a close affectionate relationship with her dad. Now the thought that she might lose him struck her hard. She was tempted to pack a bag, get in the car and drive straight up to Exeter to see for herself, but then there was Thomas to consider. She couldn't leave a baby and a very young child with a man she had only just started to live with even if he was a doctor and anyway he had his practice to consider. Margaret couldn't manage on her own that was for sure. She could always take the kids with her of course but the hospital visiting would be difficult so in the end she decided to wait for further news from her mother.

When Sam woke on Boxing Day she felt a sense of foreboding engulf her. Simon, a sensitive man, recognised something of her state of mind and acted accordingly, feeding the kids and keeping them accupied. Sam was tempted to ring her mother for news while at the same time only too aware that she would be the first to hear had there been any significant change in her father's condition. As the day wore on she lost patience and rang anyway. Anything was better than sitting around fearing the worst.

The news wasn't good. Her father was suffering severe respiratory distress and the doctors were considering whether he should be placed on a ventilator. The poor man was tired and weak with no appetite and a high temperature and the antibiotics didn't appear to be working. That was enough for Sam. "I'll come home mum not that I will be much use but at least you'll have someone at your side."

Maggie made feeble noises of protest but the die was cast. Beneath those protests Sam thought she could detect relief at the prospect of her daughter being with her to share the burden. Sam asked Blaise if she would mind Simon looking after her for a couple of days while she visited her grandad who was very ill in hospital. The little girl didn't mind at all and even offered to look after Thomas while Sam was in Exeter. The offer was smilingly declined. Of course she would take the baby with her leaving with reassurances from Simon that he would hold the fort and ring her each night to give and take news.

Once the decision was made Sam set out as soon as she could pack her bags. The journey was over 200 miles but Thomas liked the motion of being driven in the car and was a good as gold until he began to get hungry. It was only then that they stopped at motorway service station for Sam to feed the baby and take a short rest. On the resumption of the journey the baby fell asleep in his carrycot almost at once so the rest of the trip was easy and peaceful.

It had been agreed with Maggie that they would meet first at home rather than at the hospital. When they did meet up Sam was shocked by her mother's appearance. She looked worn out and worried. She hugged her daughter for a long restorative while before turning her attention to her grandson. "Beautiful child. Hello Thomas I'm your gran."

Seeing the baby appeared to bring back a sparkle of life to Maggie's tired eyes

Just for that moment Sam recognised the pure love of generation to generation before she returned to the practicalities of why they were there. "How is he mum?"

"Not good darling. He's coughing his heart out, finding it hard to breath and they've put him on a ventilator now which is not a good sign." She produced a short sharp laugh. He cheered up though when he heard his daughter and grandson were coming to visit."

"Let me have a cup of tea and give the baby some milk then we'll all go and see him in hospital."

Sam had always hated hospitals, hated the lingering antiseptic smell, hated the atmosphere which seemed to be one of gloom enlightened by bursts of forced smiles and uncomfortable shifting about in the chairs provided for visitors who couldn't wait to get away or alternatively longed for their loved one to show signs of feeling better, maybe frustrated at not being able to help.

When Trylon saw Sam and the baby come into the ward with Maggie he lifted the face mask to smile a greeting. Sam was shocked by how haggard her dad looked and dismayed by the knowledge that there was going nothing she could do to help him. He wasn't old by contemporary standards, but that night he looked very old and indeed weary. Sam's heart went out to him. She kissed his leathery cheek and introduced him to his grandson. That seemed to bring life back into that tired face. In fact they were lucky to be there. The ward sister had advised strongly against taking babies into the ward and it was only when she explained that her father had never seen his grandson that she relented with a stern, "Five minutes, no more." Whether that was because she thought there may never be another opportunity or what Sam wasn't sure.

The sister stuck to her word and hurried them away after the stipulated five minutes. Maggie asked Sam to wait in the car while she went back to speak to Trylon again on her own. After about ten minutes a knock on the car window signalled Maggie's return.

"Be an angel would you darling, go on home, look after the baby. I'm going to stay here for the night to keep Trylon company." She handed over the carkeys, her face creased in worry.

Of course Sam did as she was told. The house was as she had always remembered it, her own room virtually the same as when she'd left home to go to university yet without her parents in it there was an emptiness which she hated. It was going to be a long night. Thomas didn't appear to be affected by the atmosphere the way Sam felt and after his feed he went to sleep almost at once. The journey must have tired him out. Now, with all the things that needed to be done, done, Sam felt the weight of time on her shoulders. She feared for the father she had always doted on, wishing she could be at his bedside to share in the vigil with Maggie.

Sam didn't go to bed but anyway fell asleep on the sofa. Thomas wasn't the only one to be tired out after the journey. She woke in a daze, uncertain where she was and why she was there. It was the plaintive cries of the baby that woke her. When she glanced at her watch she saw it was gone eight o'clock. No wonder the baby was crying. She changed him all the while apologising to the child for her neglect. She fed him a messy breakfast, half cereal, half milk. Then she went upstairs to take a shower after which, feeling human again, she made tea and toast. She was very hungry and only when she was through her third slice of toast did she remember that she hadn't eaten at all the previous evening.

When Sam rang Maggie on her mobile she sensed the worry in her mother's voice, worry about the fate of her very dear partner. Some might have described Trylon as an awkward man both in physical actions and in social connections but to Maggie he would always be that kind and gentle friend she had loved since the day she'd met him. The thought that she might lose him was just too terrible to conceive. This led her, at least on the surface, to present a confident and hopeful manner with regard to Trylon's sickness. "I think he had a better night sweetheart and I'm sure seeing you and the baby again would do him the world of good if that ward sister will let you."

So here she was in the hospital again, Thomas all wrapped up against the cold, half asleep oblivious to his surroundings. Despite the love that abounded around the hospital bed it was a difficult meeting. Trylon found it difficult to talk although he did his level best to join in the family conversation. Maggie was shattered after her night long vigil. Sam did her best, telling her dad about Simon and his grandaughter which brought weak smiles to the sick man's face.

Eventually when Thomas showed signs of restlessness, Trylon insisted that Maggie go home and have a break. Nothing was going to happen if she took some much needed respite for a few hours.

"What do you think Sam. How did he look to you?"

"Obviously very tired and that mask didn't help did it?" Thomas was asleep in his carrycot. Tears began to roll down Maggie's cheeks. Sam opened her arms and the two of them hugged deeply for a long while.

"Just what is the prognosis mum?"

"Oh you know what doctors are like, difficult to get a straight answer out of them. The ventilator does seem to be helping. They're giving him antibiotics intravenously and antivirals to try to relieve his coughing. From what I can gather the critical point will be the day after tomorrow. The infection will then either be resolved or there could be complications."

That made one decision clear for Sam. It wasn't fair to leave Simon to look after Blaise for long, but she would stay and support her mother until they knew one way or another how her father's infection was going to work out. For the next two days Maggie spent most of the time at her husband's bedside while Sam explored some of her old Exeter haunts, all the while telling a docile baby about her own childhood. Thomas behaved himself for the most part although on the second day of being wheeled round the city in his buggy he began to show signs of boredom, preferring to be back at Maggie's house crawling round on the carpet and playing with his toys.

They took Trylon off the ventilator after those two worrying days, the verdict appearing to be that he'd passed the crisis point and was now all set for recovery. Sam went in to say goodbye and to give him the chance to meet his grandson again before making a start on her long journey back home to Matchstick Cottage. When she'd gone into the hospital her dad still looked worn out although he was able to smile at the baby and say how happy he was to see Sam. She was reluctant to leave so soon but she had Blaise to consider and of course Simon.

A long journey, an irritable baby, the endless miles, until at last she reached her destination. It was good to be home, good to have Blaise in her arms, good to be spoiled by Simon as he bustled round, making her something to eat and drink, and taking care of the baby. Yet under that relief, and even joy, there remained worry about her father. Alrigh,t they said he was on the way to recovery yet when she saw him in hospital to say her goodbyes he still looked far from well. There was a strong bond between her and Trylon and the thought of possibly losing him had come as a harsh shock to Sam. True she had her own family responsibilities yet still worried that she shouldn't have left her dad so soon.

Of course she rang Maggie to tell her of her safe arrival and to ask about Trylon, yet still the worry remained. She went to bed that night and did sleep deeply, exhaustion powerful enough to overcome those worries about her dad and what she might or might not have done. It was eight o'clock in the morning when the call came. The children had been fed, she was about to set off to deposit them, Thomas with dear old Agnes Dalgetty, and Blaise at nursery school. A tearful Maggie sobbed out the message that Trylon had relapsed during the night and died at five o'clock that morning.

Sam felt as though she'd been struck by a tenton truck. The guilt at having left her father when she knew he was far from well was intense enough to leave her stunned. Simon had already left for his surgery. She felt so alone, almost desperate in her grief. Blaise was tugging at her skirt, saying they should go. Agnes had just arrived to collect the baby and all she could do was weep.

Agnes stepped into the breach, offering to take Blaise to nursery school and then take Thomas off her hands for the rest of the day. Left alone Sam was in a daze, undecided about what to do. Her mother needed support, but she was over 200 miles away in Exeter and she had her own very young family to think about. Should she undertake that long drive again that very day, should she collect the children and take them with her.

As a first move she rang Simon. Whatever she decided she needed someone here to provide support. Simon, as she expected was a rock, promising to come home as soon as he could even if it meant passing on some of his patients to Margaret Hampton.

"Thank you Simon. I can imagine how difficult it must be for you to leave at short notice."

By the time Simon got back to Matchstick Cottage Sam was back in control of her emotions, yet what Simon saw was dishevelled hair, tear-stained cheeks and puffy eyes. He took her in his arms and held her tightly to his chest. "I'm so sorry sweetheart. I thought your dad was on the mend."

"So did we all," she sobbed. "My mum is devastated. I really should go and be with her but I don't know what to do about the kids."

"Agnes and I can look after them for a while. Don't worry about it, we'll cope."

Sam loved him for his caring offer but then there was work to consider, cases in process and so on. She knew Carl would understand and accept the situation but nevertheless she felt guilty of neglect. And what could she do in Exeter? Support her mother of course, help with the funeral arrangements and so on, but she would miss her babies even for a few short days. To take them with her in the circumstances would be unfair on them. My God, life was difficult at times. At that moment in time indecision was a plague on her mind.

"You're a lovely man Simon and I love you deeply."

And now she dried her tears and packed a bag. Her mum and dad had always gone out of their way to support her throughout her whole life. The very least she could do now was to support Maggie in her hour of grief. She was still tired from her previous journey, but buoyed by a new resolve of love and duty she started on the road to Exeter once again promising to ring home as soon as she got there. Already there was a sense of absence in the house, the ghost of Trylon was everywhere around them in objects reminding them of the dead husband and father. Maggie was inconsolable and Sam felt an inadequate source of comfort although she did her very best to help her mother cope with her grief.

Chapter 25

It was Maggie's turn to feel guilty. "You shouldn't have driven all that way my darling. I could have coped."

They clung together for a while until Maggie disentangled herself to make them both a much needed cup of tea. As they sat either side of the kitchen table drinking their tea a hiatus loomed between them. Grief took people in various ways. Now it was as though neither mother nor daughter knew what to say next.

Finally Maggie did break the spell. "I shall so miss him Sam. Such a gentle kind man, he didn't deserve to go so soon. I thought we would just grow old together sitting in our rocking chairs and reminiscing, not that we have any rocking chairs." She smiled wanly. "You know it's the space really that I worry about. What's going to fill that space that Trylon occupied? Almost everything I did involved reference to him and now there's just space where he used to be."

"I miss him too mum, and my kids have lost their granddad. I think you should come down to Kent and live with us. I'm sure Simon would be happy to have you live with us."

"You must be joking love. I don't want to spend the rest of my life as the little old lady sitting in the corner getting in everyone's way. I have lots of friends here in

Exeter, lots of things to do, the film club, my bridge nights although I'll need a new partner now." Again the wan smile as she struggled to come to terms with life as a widow.

Sam sighed, shook her head but was there relief at the back of her mind. She loved Maggie very much indeed but to have her living in the same household would upset the scheme of things as they were. She would have lived up to her offer of course but her mother's refusal averted what might have been problematic in the long run.

"Mum, I'm a mess, dirty and tired. Would you mind very much if I had a bath and washed my hair?"

Later in her bathrobe sitting beside the fire, her hair wrapped in a turban, she felt more able to offer consolation to her grieving mother. They sat side by side on the sofa arms around each other, saying little but each giving the other succour in their hour of need.

"Sam I know this sounds strange but I wondered if you'd sleep in my bed tonight. I could do with the company, and the feel of a warm body by my side. If it embarrasses you forget that I asked."

"It doesn't embarrass me mum. Of course I'll share your bed. I just hope we won't keep each other awake with our sadness about dad."

The next day was a day of action. Funeral arrangements to be made, Maggie's thoughts about how she would live her life without her beloved Trylon by her side, what to do with his things. It was too early to give away all Trylon's clothes, too sudden a finality so they left things as they were for the time being at least. However between them they fixed a date for the funeral, contacted all the people concerned and booked a caterer for the sad day.

"Darling, you've been a great comfort to me, but now you should go home and look after your children. That Simon sounds like a treasure to me, but is it fair to leave him in charge any longer. Useful having a doctor in the family though," she said with a smile on her face.

So that was it, another long drive. She'd be wearing a rut in the road if this went on. It was good to be home, good to be greeted so enthusiastically by her little daughter and by Simon of course and to cuddle little Thomas in her arms although he showed no signs of having missed her.

In the days that followed she had a decision to make about her dad's funeral. Who was going to attend as far as her family was concerned. Simon had already said he would take some outstanding leave and go with her. Then there were the kids. Maggie had told her that Trylon had expressed a wish to be buried rather than cremated so that meant standing out in probably cold weather so the baby was out. Blaise would not want to be left out whatever the weather. She was a precocious little girl, eager to participate in anything that was going. In her own childish way she had loved the man she'd called grandpa, feeling sad because she knew that was how she *should* feel although perhaps more excited by the thought of a visit to her gras than upset.

In the end Sam asked Agnes Dalgetty to look after Thomas for a couple of days, a request that she was only too delighted to fulfil.

The day of the funeral dawned murky and cold. The vicar, Charles Doggert, had known Trylon and Maggie personally so his sermon rang true so providing some small solace for Maggie and Sam. It was bitterly cold at the grave side. Sam worried that she shouldn't have let Blaise attend. In fact the little girl took it all in her stride snuggling into her mother's side as the ritual progressed.

Nevertheless Sam was glad to get her back in the warm when they all went back to the house to reminisce and have something to eat and drink. Blaise was in her element being spoiled by all and sundry forgetting perhaps that this was a sad occasion, that she would never see her grandpa again.

In Sam's eyes Maggie was magnificent. She must have been feeling like shit inside, yet there she was, dry eyed, talking to everyone, making sure they had a drink and some food, circulating round the room like a hostess at any other social gathering. At one point Sam did catch her standing motionless at the kitchen door, a trance-like look on her face, but then as soon as she saw Sam looking her way, she snapped back into action and continued as before.

Simon had blended well into the family scene, chatting with friends and relations of Trylon and Maggie, making them tactfully aware of who he was and why he was there. Seeing Sam alone for a moment he came across the room to drape an arm casually round her waist. "Your mum's great Sam, handling it all so well and appearing to keep her spirits up despite what I'm sure she's feeling underneath. You know I wouldn't mind if she came down to live with us. She'd be great for the kids."

Sam leant over to give him a kiss on the cheek. "That's sweet of you Simon, but she loves this house and has lots of friends locally, a whole way of life which she'd miss even if half of her wasn't here to enjoy it. Tell you the truth I did mention it when I was here last and she wouldn't even consider the idea. I might get her to come down for a few days though if that's alright with you."

Chapter 26

Life moved inexorably on. Sam still thought of her dad in quiet moments although now she had another of those thunderous changes of life that occurred to most people now and then. She was pregnant again or thought she was. It was a planned pregnancy, carefully considered and discussed, but none the less wonderful for all that. She had done a selftest at the office, and now could hardly contain herself with excitement. My God she thought to herself, what am I like, four kids, three fathers. She rang Simon at the surgery and in code told him the good news.

"I'll make an appointment for you with Margaret Hampton to get you checked out," he said once he could collect his delighted breath. "And we must celebrate tonight. What do you fancy for dinner? You better make the most of it sweetheart, no alcohol for you from now on."

"I'm up for that lover and talking of lovers, I love you Simon. And I know someone who will be delighted when she's told of one more baby to look after although Thomas will be a toddler by the time this one's born." After she'd made that casual remark it struck her that Simon might not have understood whether she meant Blaise or Agnes. In truth they would both be delighted so she let it stand.

For the rest of the day Sam did her work in a haze of exuberance. The people she went to see must have wondered just what cloud she was floating on. That feeling was hypedup after her appointment with Margaret Hampton who confirmed what she was already certain of, but with the added bonus of the doctor's confirmation of the state of her health. "You're becoming quite an expert at this birth thing Sam. My very best congratulations, and to Simon of course although no doubt I'll be hearing a lot from him in the coming weeks.

Blaise was over the moon when they got round to telling her although a little confused when it came to talking about half-sisters. Anyway she soon put that behind her as irrelevant leaving her with the coming excitement of having two young siblings to care for. When Sam eventually told Carl Rocklove that she was expecting another baby he made all the right noises yet there was something whimsical about his manner that told of regret and perhaps missing out. They had to work together and whatever Carl''s personal feeling might have been, he was professional enough not to let them interfere with their everyday relationship at work.

Winter passed, spring edged by and then in the summer baby Thomas became crawling Thomas and by the end of the summer toddling Thomas, all the while under the watchful guidance of Blaise. As the baby grew so did Sam's belly until she reached the point of wanting nothing else but to be relieved of the burden she was lugging around with her each day. When finally the day arrived and Simon took her into hospital Sam was happy with their decision that Simon would be with her during the birth. The period of labour was relatively short and painless although still exhausting. As she lay back, half asleep, her thoughts were blissful. Another little boy for Blaise to play with and protect.

Agnes brought Blaise and Thomas to visit in the hospital. There they all were, the perfect young family all lined up for life to come. Sam couldn't have felt happier. Then Simon returned, after a brief spell away to check his messages, to complete the happy picture.

Sam wasn't going to give up her job just because she had three young children to care for although she agreed with Simon to take a six months break, still well within the terms of her maternity leave. Not that there would've been any difficulty getting her job back anyway due to the chronic shortage of social workers. Soon a routine developed with which Sam was very happy. Blaise was taken to school, Thomas to nursery while she looked after the new baby they'd christened David. A sort of earth mother at least for six months. Agnes was always at hand if she needed to be away from home for shopping or other tasks.

Sam had wondered about the name. Was she being morbid, was she trying to reincarnate her lost little boy? She couldn't have truthfully answered that question but Simon was quite happy with the suggestion anyway.

Sam relished the experience of absolute concentration on child care, laughing when Simon, every now and then, reminded her that she had a husband too. She wasn't old by any standards yet her life so far had been so eventful her memory banks were already chockerblock and needed a rest. There had been several men in her life but now, if it was up to her, she was going to stick with lovely Simon for the remainder of her days.

Like all things that lovely period of baby care came to an end. Sam couldn't make up her mind as to whether she was glad or not. All along she had intended to go back to work after that initial period yet when the time came she felt some reluctance. She had loved being an earth mother which was how she saw herself in those first few months of David's life but another part of her yearned for the real life of her work with Carl and the others in the service. Agnes was already geared up to look after David as well taking Thomas to nursery school. Everything was falling into place for one happy family. Sam put her doubts to one side and on a cold winter morning made her way to the office to meet up with Carl Rocklove to discuss her assignments for the week.

Chapter 27

It was warm in the summer sun although where Sam sat under the willow tree beside the pond that Simon had installed to amuse the kids, she was shaded from the full glare of the sun's rays. To tell the truth she was daydreaming, half asleep lulled by the sound of the children playing in the garden. True she would have loved Simon to be here with her yet she wasn't sad. We all had to go sometime and she'd had many years of love from that dear man before he'd left her so she wasn't going to be sad.

Her thoughts fluttered like butterflies in her brain, gently weaving their way through her memory, ghosting intermittently without order or pattern. She thought back to her first love Chrisopher, the first little David's father,a disappointment perhaps but they had both been very young at the time She was enjoying the experience, here in the garden of her beloved Matchstick Cottage with her family all around. She was a lucky woman she mused. Four lovely children although then, just for an instant, grief intruded as she thought of the first David, that wonderful bright little boy granted such a short spell of life before being cruelly taken away He had missed out on a life and she still regretted that with all her soul. But then she had the three others so she was indeed a lucky woman.

And all those grandchildren she absolutely doted on. Life had been kind to her. And then the secret, although why it should be a secret she really didn't understand. Blaise had told her that her granddaughter June was pregnant and expecting a little girl in the New Year but she wasn't to breath a word of it for now.

"You alright mum?" That was her daughter Blaise now. Dear Blaise always caring Blaise, sometimes a bit too much Sam thought although you couldn't fault her for that could you? She was the same with her own children, ever the mother hen, not that her two strapping great teenagers needed much mothering these days,

After that short interruption in her daydreaming she fell back again to memories. Gentle Jason Anderson who had been so loving, yet had never been the front runner in her affections. The last time she'd seen him had been here at Matchstick Cottage many years ago. She prayed that the lovely lad had found someone to love him back and had children of his own on whom he could dote. Then in a moment her thoughts swung to that bastard Steven Bradbury. She had loved the man, had Blaise with him and yet he chose to bugger off with another woman. She had thought her heart has been broken for ever. Then of course she finally made a life with Doctor Morris. Simon Morris, definitely the love of her life. She had said to herself she wasn't going to be maudlin, yet now the hurt came. She did miss him terribly no matter she might rationalise life.

She opened one eye to see George standing by her chair, his smiling face so like his mother's. "Sorry did I wake you gran? Mum wants to know if you'd like a cup of tea but I know where there's a bottle of chilled Chardonnay which you might prefer or at least a glass of it." He grinned as though they were conspirators in some secret plot.

"You trying to lead me into bad habits young man? Anyway where's that brother of yours?"

"He's chatting up cousin Rachel, think he rather fancies her."

"Go on then, I'd love a glass of wine. No need to mention it to your mother, she thinks I drink too much anyway." She smiled fondly at the strapping lad by her side.

While George strode away across the lawn to do her bidding, she concentrated on not falling asleep before he could get back. Not all her family were gathered in that sunny garden. Thomas, who had never married despite numerous girlfriends, appearing on the scene every so often, but not here today. He was an archaeologist, at present away on some dig in the south of France. He spent a lot of his time away from his London flat, travelling all over the world wherever a site took his particular interest. Sam didn't see him or hear from him much but she still got a sharp thrill when she received a cryptic postcard from some obscure part of the world confirming he was still alive.

She never got that glass of Chardonnay because David sent Rachel to tell her that she was wanted in the house where the whole family waited to wish her a happy birthday, and to drink her health with a glass of champagne.